# CHURCH GROWTH IN SIERRA LEONE

# CHURCH GROWTH SERIES

*Church Growth in Mexico:* Donald McGavran, John Huegel, Jack Taylor

*Wildfire—Church Growth in Korea:* Roy E. Shearer

*New Patterns of Church Growth in Brazil:* William R. Read

*Church Growth in Central and Southern Nigeria:* John B. Grimley, Gordon E. Robinson

*God's Impatience in Liberia:* Joseph Conrad Wold

*Tinder in Tabasco:* Charles Bennett

*Church Growth in Sierra Leone:* Gilbert W. Olson

*Understanding Church Growth:* Donald McGavran

# CHURCH GROWTH IN SIERRA LEONE

A Study of Church Growth in Africa's Oldest
Protestant Mission Field

*by*

GILBERT W. OLSON

William B. Eerdmans Publishing Company
Grand Rapids, Michigan

4/23

Printed in the United States of America

*To the unheralded heroes of the Church:*
*the evangelists of the*
*Evangelical United Brethren Church in Sierra Leone*
*and to the evangelists and catechists of the*
*Church of Jesus Christ in Africa, Latin America,*
*Oceania, and Asia*
*I dedicate this book.*

# PREFACE

Over 150 years have passed since the first permanent Protestant missionary work began in Sierra Leone in 1811. During those years hundreds of missionaries have given their lives, millions of dollars have been spent, and countless hours of prayer have been poured out that the people of Sierra Leone might be reconciled to God through Christ — be saved from bondage to sin and superstition.

Sierra Leone was the hope of the enslaved. Slaves who assisted Britain during the American War of Independence, or who were on board slavers seized by British ships off the west coast of Africa, found freedom there. That land symbolized the end of the inhuman slave trade and was, therefore, chosen as the first mission field in Africa by several Protestant mission boards.

The mission boards hoped that as the free slaves (particularly the liberated Africans from the slave ships) became Christian they could become men of God who would evangelize Africa and win its peoples to Christ and His Church. Many liberated Africans gave substance to this hope. They became Christians and returned to their homelands taking Christianity with them. Thus the Yoruba tribe in Nigeria and the Fanti tribe in Ghana began the trek to Christ.

Having lived in the hinterland of Sierra Leone as an evangelistic missionary and having committed myself to its people that they may know Christ and become strong members of His Church, I became intensely interested in the outcome of all this missionary activity and Christian effort. This book is the result of three years' (1962-1965) research among the congregations in Sierra Leone and the records of various Missions and Churches in Africa, England, and the United States.

I discovered that although 67 per cent of the descendants of the freed slaves are Protestant Christians, only 2.1 per cent of the tribespeople are. Missions in other parts of Africa — such as southern Nigeria, southern Ghana, and Buganda —

have been far more successful. Why is Sierra Leone, the first of the Protestant mission fields in Africa, one of the slowest south of the Sahara in being discipled? What is the growth history of each denomination? What can we learn from each concerning obedience to the divine mandate? This book attempts to answer these questions.

My studies have convinced me that large sections of Sierra Leone are still winnable. At the same time, unless speedy and drastic changes of emphases are made soon, field after field will be irretrievably lost. I write with urgency.

A complex society such as that of Sierra Leone and a missionary movement of 150 years cannot be summarily described. The story must be systematically told. Before anyone can understand the problems or bright opportunities of missions in Sierra Leone, he will need to see the land and the people to whom missionaries went and among whom the Churches developed. He can then go on to study each denomination's growth history, observe the lessons to be learned, and state what must be done to win the peoples of Sierra Leone to Christ.

My heartfelt thanks go to the many missionaries and church leaders whose information, suggestions, and insights were invaluable in the preparation of this book. The account of each denomination was based on information secured from them as well as from the books and reports listed in the bibliography.

Readers should note that this book was set in type before the Evangelical United Brethren–Methodist merger. These denominations therefore are referred to by their pre-merger names.

Particular thanks go to Dr. Donald A. McGavran who guided my research, directed my studies, and gave counsel in the writing of this book; and to Dr. Alan R. Tippett, professor of the School of World Mission and Institute of Church Growth, Fuller Theological Seminary.

— GILBERT W. OLSON

# TABLE OF CONTENTS

9

# LIST OF MAPS OF SIERRA LEONE

# LIST OF GRAPHS AND TABLES

# TERMS USED IN THIS BOOK

Church    the Church of Christ universal or a denomination organized within a country.

church    a particular field within a country or wherever used as an adjective.

Mission    the mission board or society of a foreign Church or the mission organization within a country.

mission    a local congregation or wherever used as an adjective.

# PART I

## HISTORICAL AND
## SOCIOLOGICAL BACKGROUND

# CHAPTER I

# A MAGNIFICENT LABORATORY
# OF MISSIONS

Sierra Leone! This was the first Protestant mission field in tropical Africa. The first emissaries of the Church Missionary Society landed here in 1804. Here Joseph Smith, Methodist class leader in Cape Coast, was educated. From here no less than 112 African ministers went out in the first fifty years to carry the Gospel to Nigeria. From Bishopscourt, a noble edifice overlooking the Atlantic Ocean, a long succession of missionary bishops directed important missions of the Anglican Church. Here, working with freed slaves, they established, more than a hundred years ago, a thoroughly African church. Here Fourah Bay College crowned a notable educational program — a monument to the social work of Christian missions.

Yet, despite this excellent start, in what was in 1804 an almost completely animistic country, the outcome has been unsatisfactory — a curious mixture of victories and defeats. The Creole community, which arose from the freed slaves, has become solidly Christian chiefly in the Anglican and Methodist Churches. The Evangelical United Brethren have twenty thousand communicants among the tribesmen. Several small spurts of growth have occurred.

But none of the fourteen European and American missionary societies in Sierra Leone has broken through to really great growth. Only one tribe has begun to become Christian. No sweeping people movement to Christ has taken place. The tribes remain pagan, gradually becoming Moslem by needless default. The African Churches established by the missionary societies, after becoming independent of mission control, either have been sealed off in the Creole community or proved powerless to reproduce among the tribesmen. In this premier mission field, devoted mission and church work has been carried out, and God has granted many beginnings of church growth; but none has surged forward to spread the Christian faith among the common people of the land. Enormous effort has gone into the multiplication of mission schools in which the Bible is regularly taught by Christian teachers. Small churches have arisen around most schools, but have not spread to the people.

Sierra Leone is thus a magnificent laboratory for the study of church growth. Though a small land, it presents a remarkable opportunity to learn the processes of Christian mission which God blesses and the concomitants of religious change which must be recognized and used by Christian ministers and missionaries. The study of church growth here should be replete with lessons for Christian mission throughout Africa — and Asia and Latin America as well. Sierra Leone is a receptive land. The multitudes in it are not armor-plated against the Gospel, or held in subjection by powerful non-Christian religions, intense cultural antipathies, or tyrannical governments. Here the multitudes are and have been approachable. Here Churches could have grown greatly but have not. It is a good place to study mission objectively; to discover both fruitless procedures and those which effectively spread the light of the revelation of the glory of God in the face of Jesus Christ.

Thinking this, I began in 1962 investigating the growth of the Sierra Leonean Churches. I knew them first-hand. As a missionary, I had worked among Evangelical United Brethren congregations in the Mende country and had visited churches of other denominations and fields of other missions. On my way home I spent some time in the mission archives at various mission headquarters in England and America. At the Fuller Seminary School of World Mission I studied many cases of church growth and the anthropological principles which illuminate innovation and social change. Then I carefully put together the pertinent pieces of evidence bearing on the growth and non-growth of many different denominations in this West African land.

In brief, the conclusions coming out of the laboratory, for which the rest of the book will present the evidence, are these: (a) In Sierra Leone great discipling is now possible and is God's will. However, despite much church and mission activity, little discipling occurs. For example, most of the Mende tribe could be, but is not being, won for Christ. (b) The Churches in Sierra Leone would grow more soundly and more rapidly if the policies and methods suggested herein were to be enacted. (c) These policies and methods are biblically desirable and in many lands have yielded sound and rapid church growth.

Any serious investigation of Christian mission is based on some theory of mission and some philosophy of mission work. My *theory of mission* has four basic principles. First, the primary purpose of the Church and her missions is the winning of persons and groups of persons to Christ and forming them into vital growing congregations. If we divide the work of missions into discipling and perfecting, then the first step is to disciple individuals and groups. The second is to perfect them, i.e., lead them to become responsible members of Christ's Church. Discipling precedes perfecting. Men and tribes must become His followers before they will "learn all things whatsoever" He has commanded.

Second, the growth of the Church is the surest way to bring about the liberating rule of God in society. God's rule in Sierra Leone will bring men into open discipleship to Jesus Christ and reform and elevate the social order and all its institutions: family life, village customs, intertribal harmony, education, economy, urbanization, and government. As men become Christians, the reconstruction of society among humane and productive lines becomes more and more possible. The growth of the Church is a necessary forerunner to major advance in social structure.

Third, in countries such as Sierra Leone (and there are many of them in Asia and Africa) where society exists as tribes, clans, extended families, and castes, multi-individual conversion (loosely, group conversion) is the soundest mode of mission. Mission theory must not be confined to winning individuals, but rather enlarged to require winning groups of persons. As Kenneth Scott Latourette said thirty years ago,

> More and more we must dream in terms of winning groups, not merely individuals. Too often, with our Protestant, nineteenth century individualism we have torn men and women, one by one out of the family, village, or clan, with the result

that they have been permanently de-racinated and malad-justed (1963: 159).

Anthropology has shown us that men respond to the Gospel in different ways, according to their social background and customary ways of making decisions on their own initiative. This is a phenomenon of modern civilization. In the West, when Christians evangelize, they call on individuals to believe on Jesus Christ. This method of individual evangelism was brought to Sierra Leone by the first missionaries. The result was slow discipling.

Most men of Asia and Africa are accustomed to making decisions as families or clans, or as villages or chiefdoms. This is true in rural Sierra Leone, where a group of people deciding to follow Christ touch off a chain reaction among other groups. This people movement does not mean that everyone within each group becomes Christian at the same time. Rather, it means that a sufficient number of a group has decided to follow Christ, so that the Bible becomes the group's book and Christianity becomes the group's religion (McGavran 1955).

The people movement method of winning people to Christ is the quickest and soundest way of discipling and perfecting people. It is the quickest way because through it larger numbers of people turn to Christ and become members of His Church than through the individual method. But more important, *the people movement method is the soundest way* because each convert comes into the Church with his family and intimates. The individual method, by way of contrast, tends to extract and alienate the convert from his family and in-group so that he has little or no influence upon his community, either to win others to Christ or to change customs which are evil. Further, he is more subject to temptations from the mass of animism around him and from the social pressures of non-Christians.

A people movement, on the other hand, being the joint decision of a number of individuals comprising some section of a society, be it five families or five hundred, enables converts to become Christian without social alienation while remaining in full contact with their non-Christian relatives. This enables other groups, across the years, after suitable instruction, to come to a Christian decision and form Christian churches.

When the number of groups becomes large enough, the Christians can also change tribal customs which are incompatible with Christianity. Thus the deeper commitment of members within a people movement has far-reaching implications.

Other reasons why people movements are the soundest way of discipling and perfecting people are: (1) The group and its natural leaders come into the church together and give the church greater stability. (2) People movements are more likely to be self-supporting and less dependent upon the mission and the missionary than Christians who are converted one by one. (3) Christians converted through people movements are more likely to stand up under persecution, for conviction is buttressed by social cohesion. (4) People movements provide better church discipline because the discipline comes from the social pressure of friends and relatives.

Growth in quality and quantity can and normally do go together. Church growth includes both horizontal growth in numbers won to Christ, and vertical growth in depth of commitment of these people to God and to the way of Christ. Ideally, these two operate conjunctively, because growth only in numbers produces baptized pagans; growth only in "quality" leads to sterility and dead churches — keeping the form of Christianity but lacking the power of Christ.

The kind of church growth for which I plead emphasizes conversion of the whole man in all his relationships and bears the following characteristics:

1. It wins converts and forms them into churches.
2. The churches multiply, i.e., plant other churches.
3. Physical growth is accompanied by deepening spiritual commitment.
4. The fruit of this growing experience is seen in society at large, e.g., by Christianizing social customs, by social service, and by bringing others into abundant life in Christ.

It is easy to recognize numerical growth, but not so easy to appraise depth in commitment to God and the way of Christ. Each person has his own idea of what "quality" is and how "Christian" a person, or a group of persons, is. The selection of criteria for appraisal will greatly affect the choice of methods employed to disciple the tribes. Some missionaries and the national leaders whom they have trained have so confused western ethos and civilization with Christianity that they feel a person who does not behave in a western manner must therefore not be a Christian. For such leaders "quality" means being civilized, and they depend heavily upon schools to win people to Christ because only schools can yield such "quality" Christians. Further, such leaders often demand a standard of religious quality not practiced by many Christians in the West. They forget that it has taken generations for the West to achieve its present standard of Christianization, and that much of western ethos is merely cultural and morally neutral.

Western ethos must not be used as a criterion for judging the spiritual "quality" of Christians. Instead, the following criteria should be used: (1) frequency in attending services; (2) growth in the knowledge of the Bible and in the knowledge of what it means to be a follower of Christ; (3) willingness to assume responsibility in the church; (4) the new life in Christ morally higher than the old life (rather than compared with "ideal" western life), and (5) zeal in winning other people to Christ.

The philosophy of mission work described above applies to the whole gamut of mission activities and asks what each work should be in light of the great goal: the extension of Christ's liberating rule and His Church. All activities — evangelistic, revivalistic, benevolent, and organizational — must be evaluated to determine how effectively they advance the enterprise toward the goal. If any activity is contributing little or nothing to the advance, it should be modified, relocated, or dropped. We must reject works which, under today's conditions, neither issue in nor give hope of issuing in church multiplication.

Churches and missions carry on many activities and programs. They provide medical services; operate schools; develop communities; maintain institutions for training lay and clerical leaders; station, supervise, and pay evangelists; construct youth camps; preach; baptize, and administer holy communion. All these activities are unquestionably good.

But what is the relationship of each to the growth of the Church? How well has the Church grown numerically, spiritually, organically? How many converts has each of these activities yielded? How spiritually vital are such converts?

For example, medical services operated by missions have been a boon to many people. Motivated by the compassion of Christ, mission medicine is intended not only to heal people, but also to convey the idea that God loves them and that they ought to turn to Him by accepting Christ as their Savior and entering the Church. But to what extent has this program, in receptive populations such as those of Sierra Leone, brought persons to Christ and led them to be responsible members of His Church? If the extent is small, how may the program be changed so that spiritual healing may accompany the physical? Furthermore, how can this compassion of the rich foreigners become an expression of the local churches?

Again, what about schools? Schools have often been the main activity of the mission and church and a means of reaching into new areas. But what is the result of such activity? Many Sierra Leoneans have been educated, but what percentage of children and youth have become responsible members of the Church? To what extent has the school system helped or hindered the emergence of leadership from among the uneducated in village congregations and town churches? If the school system has not yielded the amount of growth and leadership expected from it, how can it be changed so that it will become a greater means of evangelization and church planting?

What about evangelists and ministers? What are the roles played by each? To what extent are they evangelizing whole chiefdoms and planting churches in all their villages? How effective or ineffective is the system of foreign-paid church leaders?

The fourteen Churches and their assisting missions furnish the student of missionary expansion many different patterns of mission work and church growth. The activities carried on by the different Churches and missions, or by the same Church or mission in different periods of its history, may be regarded as experiments in mission. As I describe the development of each of the fourteen Churches, the extent to which policy and actual practice shaped it, and the state in which it exists today, the reader may in imagination proceed from experiment to experiment and note to what degree each Church has achieved, or failed to achieve, the purposes for which it was begun.

The main purpose for which all missions in Sierra Leone were established, for which life was poured out over the last hundred and sixty years, is well expressed in the statement of aims drawn up at the formation of the Church Missionary Society in 1797:

> It is a duty highly incumbent upon every Christian to endeavor to propagate the knowledge of the Gospel.... The persons present at this meeting do form themselves into a Society for that purpose.

Three kinds of church growth will be described: numerical, spiritual, and organic. Numerical growth will be shown in the line of graphs; spiritual and organic growth will be discussed in the descriptions of the various denominations. As we proceed through the laboratory, I shall indicate the areas where change is needed and will point out how this change should be accomplished if sounder and greater growth is to take place.

But before the Missions and Churches can be understood, a word about the land of Sierra Leone and its peoples will be necessary.

# CHAPTER 2

# THE LAND AND ITS PEOPLE

## CLIMATE AND TOPOGRAPHY

Sierra Leone, lying on the west coast of Africa 7°-10° north of the equator, is tropical with a mean temperature of about 80° Fahrenheit and two seasons, wet and dry. The heaviest rain is from July to September, the rice-growing season, and the driest season is from December to March. Joining these two seasons are heavy, short rainstorms in the night, becoming more frequent approaching July and tapering off from October to November.

Most of the country has been cleared for rice farming, the main occupation. Farming is done on a system of bush-fallow rotation. Each year the farmer must select three to ten acres of secondary forest in which to do his farming — the older the forest, the better its fertility. The forest is then cut, dried, and burned. Stumps are left so that the forest may grow back quickly afer harvest. The thicker felled trees not consumed by the fire are also left. After one or two years they make excellent firewood.

Planting is done by broadcast sowing, followed by back-bending hoeing with short-handled hoes. In the growing season the women weed while the men make fences and set traps to keep out animals. As the grain appears the children use sling-shots to keep birds away. Men and women work together to harvest the rice, using a paring knife to harvest the heads. The straw is left in the fields. Most of the farming is done by the farmer himself for local consumption. However, some cocoa, coffee, ginger, and oil palm kernels are grown for export. In the north, agriculture tends to give way to cattle husbandry.

Much of the country's wealth is now derived from its

23

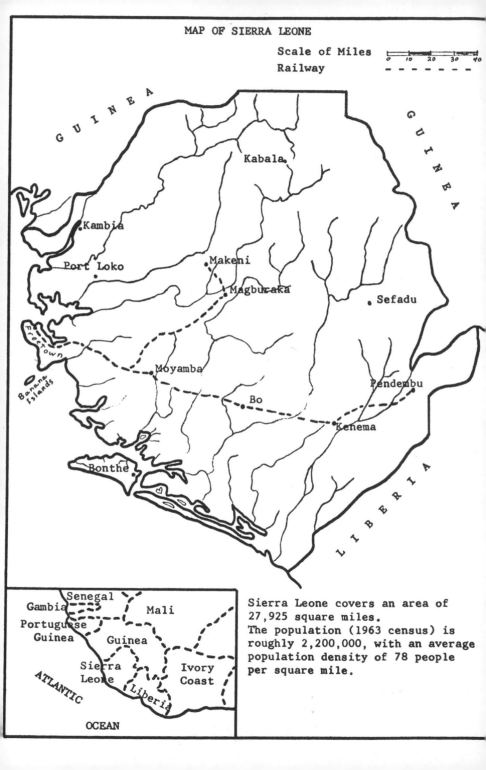

MAP OF SIERRA LEONE

Scale of Miles

Railway

GUINEA

GUINEA

Kabala

Kambia

Port Loko

Makeni

Magburaka

Sefadu

Freetown

Moyamba

Banana Islands

Pendembu

Bo

Kenema

Bonthe

LIBERIA

Senegal

Gambia

Mali

Portuguese
Guinea

Guinea

Sierra
Leone

Ivory
Coast

ATLANTIC

Liberia

OCEAN

Sierra Leone covers an area of
27,925 square miles.
The population (1963 census) is
roughly 2,200,000, with an average
population density of 78 people
per square mile.

mineral resources. Alluvial diamonds are being mined over a wide area in the eastern part of the country and are causing diamond rushes and boom towns. The eastern section also contains deposits of iron ore, chromite, and gold, as well as deposits of other minerals which are not being mined. The deposits of iron ore being mined are in isolated hills in the western part of the country. Near the coast large deposits of rutile have been found and mining has just begun.

## POPULATION  ~tribes & languages

Sierra Leone has many tribes, each with its own language and customs, although the Temne have largely displaced and assimilated the Bullom, and the Mende the Sherbro and Krim. (See map showing tribal distribution on page 26.)

The Western Area (the peninsula on which Freetown is situated — formerly the "Colony") is populated by descendants of the early settlers and liberated Africans, called Creoles. But the tribal immigrants from the rest of the country now greatly outnumber them. The only *lingua franca* in Sierra Leone as a whole is a form of pidgin English which is used only near the railroads and motor roads.

In the north, west, and south most of the tribes have come under the influence of Islam (see map showing religious distribution on page 46). But despite this and the efforts of hundreds of Christian missionaries for over a century and a half, the country remains predominantly animistic.

## HISTORY

*Islam animism & Christianity*

The word "war" describes the early history of Sierra Leone from before A.D. 1000 to the close of the nineteenth century, when England took complete control of the country and enforced peace. The wars were between chiefdoms of the same tribe and between tribes. Reasons for the wars ranged from retaliation, to gaining more land and power, to capturing slaves. Fear and privation reigned.

Slavery was common before the Europeans came, but the large demands of the Europeans for slaves greatly increased the number of slave raids. The Europeans themselves did not

*slaves were taken*
*Amistad*

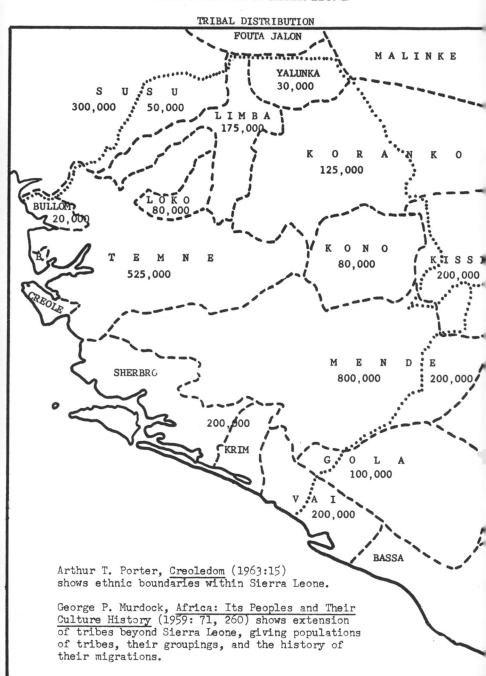

TRIBAL DISTRIBUTION

FOUTA JALON

MALINKE

YALUNKA
30,000

S U S U
300,000    50,000

L I M B A
175,000

K O R A N K O
125,000

L O K O
80,000

BULLOM
20,000

K O N O
80,000

B

T E M N E
525,000

KISSI
200,000

CREOLE

M E N D E
800,000    200,000

SHERBRO

200,000

KRIM

G O L A
100,000

V A I
200,000

BASSA

Arthur T. Porter, Creoledom (1963:15)
shows ethnic boundaries within Sierra Leone.

George P. Murdock, Africa: Its Peoples and Their
Culture History (1959: 71, 260) shows extension
of tribes beyond Sierra Leone, giving populations
of tribes, their groupings, and the history of
their migrations.

go slave raiding. They merely kept to the coast and bought slaves from the various tribes.

In the mid-1400s Portuguese sailors reached West Africa. They were trying to find a route to India. They named the peninsula, now known as the Western Area, Serra Lyon (mountain lion). The shape of the mountains and the rumbling thunder in them perhaps reminded them of lions (lions have never been plentiful in Sierra Leone). Through the centuries the name has changed to Sierra Leone, pronounced without the final e. At first the name applied only to the peninsula. Later, after numerous treaties between the British and the chiefs, the name included more and more territory until the boundaries were fixed with Liberia and France.

The Portuguese traders brought European manufactured goods to the coastal tribes in exchange for slaves and ivory. Some settled and married local women. In the early 1600s English traders licensed by the Crown began to visit Sierra Leone. They came for camwood dye, ivory, and slaves. Many European adventurers came hoping to make a fortune in the slave trade. As a result, the coastal people became accustomed to Europeans. Some chiefs even sent their sons to England for education.

The greatest effect of the slave trade and other trade upon the people was to retard progress and development. The constant threat of slave raids and wars kept the people from making any plans for progress. It became cheaper and easier to buy manufactured goods such as tools and clothes from Europeans than to make them for themselves. As a result, many arts and skills, including the making of pottery, brass, copperware, and cloth deteriorated or even died out.

It was not until the end of the 1700s that British people began to see the evil of slavery and the slave trade. The first anti-slavery law came in 1772 when all slaves in England became free men. However, many of those freed were unable to find employment and became a problem to the English authorities. Slaves who fought for the British in the War of American Independence were also freed, and as they could not go back to the United States they became a problem.

One solution tried was to send them to Africa. Sierra Leone was chosen. In 1787, 377 people (most of them Negro) were landed near what is now Freetown. They were a sorry lot. Most of them had been unemployed and were beggars. With them were some white prostitutes. The group was unable to organize itself, and in 1789, after two years, the experiment ended when the colony was attacked and burned and the settlers scattered. Two years later, 1790, sixty-four of them were found and resettled on Forah Bay under the supervision of the Sierra Leone Company.

In 1792, 1175 Loyalist Negroes from Nova Scotia arrived in Sierra Leone. These, however, had been screened so that only the most competent Negroes were allowed to come. Eight years later, in 1800, the Maroons arrived. They were freed slaves from Jamaica, in the West Indies, who had rebelled and had been shipped to Nova Scotia. (Hereafter, these three groups — those of the first experiment, the Nova Scotians, and the Maroons — shall be referred to as Settlers.) They were culturally western in dress, food, habits, and speech. They did not mingle socially with the indigenous Africans around them; nor were they encouraged to do so.

In 1807 the slave trade became illegal for British subjects. Since the Sierra Leone Company was financially a failure and was unable to cope with the slave trade, a year later, in 1808, Sierra Leone became a crown colony. From it the Royal Navy would hunt and capture slaves, bring them to Freetown, and unload the human cargo. Forty thousand Negroes, most of them from Yoriba and Ibo tribes in Nigeria, were thus freed and settled in the Colony during a period of over fifty years. (Hereafter, these shall be referred to as liberated Africans.) Through the intensive efforts of Christian missionaries these pagan, socially uprooted immigrants assumed western culture and Christianity.

At first the Settlers remained aloof from the liberated Africans. But gradually, as the latter became more and more wealthy, educated, western, and Christian, the difference between the two blurred until, after one hundred years, they had become one homogeneous unit called Creoles.

In 1896, according to agreement with France and Liberia but without consulting the chiefs, Britain declared the hinterland of Sierra Leone a Protectorate under British rule. The boundaries with French West Africa and Liberia were not drawn according to chiefdom or tribal boundaries but according to line of latitude and river watersheds. Thus some chiefdoms and tribes were divided, part British and part French.

Rather than annexing the country to the Colony and trying to force British law on the people, the governor proclaimed a Protectorate in which the chiefs would rule according to customary law but guided by British district commissioners. His hope was to have a government which would ensure peace and open the whole Protectorate to trade. The trade in turn would help the people make money, thus enabling them to improve their standard of living.

The extra administration meant more expense. Since the goal was to help the Protectorate people, the governor felt they should help pay for it, and set a tax of five shillings per year per house. The chiefs were outraged over the arrangement in which they were never even consulted. Why should they pay for a government for which they had neither asked nor wanted? Nor did they understand the tax. They thought the government had taken ownership of their houses and was charging them rent. Already the people were suffering under frontier police, called Frontiers, who harassed the tribesmen and chiefs, even to replacing chiefs with their own friends. Everywhere the chiefs saw indications that their authority was at an end. Now they feared the tax would take their houses.

This caused two wars in 1898, two years later, jointly called the Hut Tax War. The first was Bai Bureh's War in the Port Loko area. It was a war of defense in which the chiefs tried to maintain their authority over the land. Nearly one hundred towns and villages were burned by British troops (Afro-West Indians under European officers) before Bai Bureh's resistance was broken.

The Mende War (in which Vai, Loko, Temne, Bullom, and Susu also took part) was a war of retaliation. The Frontiers had burned houses and villages and fired on gatherings of men in their efforts to collect tax.

Christopher Fyfe, in *A Short History of Sierra Leone*, relates:

> Suddenly on April 27th the people rose. The government was taken completely by surprise. The rising had been planned secretly in a special Poro (secret society meeting),

and outsiders knew nothing about it. The many grievances against the new government, against the cruel Frontiers, against the Creole traders who for many decades had lorded it over them, broke in a wave of fury against all aliens. Every European and Creole was to be destroyed, all government servants, and those who had adopted European ways — every man in trousers, it was said, every woman in a dress. All over the Mende, Bullom, and Krim countries unsuspecting traders and their families were seized and hacked to death.... Missionaries, Creoles and Europeans, suffered with the rest.... The war also served as an excuse for settling personal grudges. Unpopular chiefs, particularly those friendly to the government, were killed (1962: 143-145).

By the beginning of the rains, two months later, the war was over. When the British columns went out (many of them were Temne from Yoni Chiefdom) they met little resistance. The Mende fought in disorganized bands, armed only with clubs and cutlasses. They were no match for trained soldiers.

After the short war the tax was continued and was paid. Some chiefs charged more than the five shillings and kept the balance. The Frontiers continued their harassment and took revenge for their friends killed in the war. However, in 1901 court messengers replaced the Frontiers. In 1903 each chiefdom was ruled by a tribal authority — that is, by the paramount chief and his subchiefs — but under the supervision of the district commissioners and court messengers. Chiefs convicted of oppression were replaced by successors approved by the government.

Because of the high white mortality rate it was decided in 1865 to educate Africans (Creoles) to take over administration in all the British colonies of West Africa. But the power of the Creoles was short lived. Medical discoveries lowered the white mortality rate, so the British gradually pushed the Creoles out of the senior posts. Color had higher seniority than qualification. The Creoles also lost business as Europeans began to take over the large scale trading and the Lebanese the small scale.

After the second world war Sierra Leone shared in the desire of all colonies to be self-governing. The British government then changed its policy and began an educational program to prepare the colonies for self-government. By then many tribesmen were as well educated as the Creoles. The Creoles knew that in a general election the overwhelming majority of the tribespeople would take over the country unless the dual system of government (Colony and Protectorate) were to continue. The Creoles hoped to be in charge of the Colony.

But in 1950 Dr. Milton Margai founded the Sierra Leone Peoples Party (SLPP) and demanded that the 1947 constitution establishing only one government for the country be introduced at once. In the ensuing election the SLPP won overwhelmingly, and political power bypassed the Creoles.

Movements toward independence then moved rapidly. On April 27, 1961, Sierra Leone became an independent state within the Commonwealth and subsequently became the hundredth member of the United Nations.

## EDUCATION

Until the middle of the 1800s the British government did not provide public education. Churches and private organizations ran the schools. This was true not only for Britain but also for its colonies, including the Colony of Sierra Leone (the present Western Area). Thus the first schools in Sierra Leone were begun by the Settlers from Nova Scotia who were English-speaking and, for the most part, Christian.

In the meantime the first Protestant mission in Africa was opened in 1804 by the Church Missionary Society among the Susu, just north of Sierra Leone on the Rio Pangos River. Their work (in accord with their civilizing theory of mission) was a school, but without religious services either in the school or outside. The mission lasted ten years, until 1814. By that year the number of Africans liberated in Sierra Leone had reached ten thousand, one thousand of them children. Because of the great need, the governor urged the Church Missionary Society to come and help. (The British Methodists had already sent schoolmasters in 1811.)

In response to his plea, two years later (1816) four couples were sent out as schoolmasters, schoolmistresses, and catechists. They were not sent to preach. The Society told them:

> You must keep in view, that it is the wish and determination of the Society, to provide, with the blessing of God,

Christian Education for the entire population of the Colony and its more immediate Vicinity. . . . Your direct business is with children and youth. . . . You are not Missionaries, sent to preach the Gospel; but you will become most efficient Missionaries, by your influence on all around you, if you maintain, by the Grace of God, a Character worthy of the Gospel.

Such a character will give weight to all those efforts which you may make, without departing from your proper sphere of duty to promote the good of all around you. While your time and labour are chiefly engaged in the instruction of children in matters of common education, and in opening their minds by constant catechizing, and thus endeavouring to lead them to the knowledge of themselves and of God, you may through them, do much for their parents, and for all adult persons. . . .

We are not backward to confess that our main hopes of being instruments of God to Africa are founded on the rising generation. The state of the Native Mind, and the habits in which the people have long indulged, are most unfavourable to their moral and religious improvement.

The Society has, therefore, resolved to spare no pains in the education of the children. The evil influence of the family and environment around the children have led the Society to look, with more confident hopes, to some plan which may wholly separate children from the influence of evil sentiments and habits. . . . It has taken measures, in consequence, to erect the Christian Institution of Sierra Leone (1816: 130).

This quotation shows the attitude of Europeans toward adult "uncivilized" Africans: that they were too debased and depraved to be educated, converted, or civilized. They believed the children and youth were the only ones malleable enough to be changed, and even this was considered doubtful unless they could be removed from the corrupting influence of their communities.

This was the attitude of the times toward the liberated Africans and natives, and it was shared by both the missionary societies in Sierra Leone and the Settlers. It set the pattern of missionary endeavor in Sierra Leone, a method of evangelization through schools for children and youth (hereafter referred to as *the school approach*), and with modifications, is the method used today in the second half of the twentieth century. Its effectiveness in planting churches among the tribal people will be discussed later when we examine the various Churches.

The school approach was one of the major reasons for success in Christianizing the liberated Africans because the Church Missionary Society and the Methodists worked among the *whole* group, providing enough education to help them adjust to the new way of life. Although they were from many different tribes and separated themselves accordingly, their common experience of being uprooted made them an artificially homogeneous unit.

The school approach was not the only reason for success. The matter of "ripeness," or readiness, has also to be considered. The liberated Africans had been uprooted from their families and social pressures and transplanted in a western culture. They wanted the influence and prestige of the Settlers. They viewed Christianity and western civilization as one, so they accepted both. But in so doing they gradually became as separate from the local tribal people as were the Settlers, until a caste-like relationship developed. For example, by 1852 the liberated Africans had been declared full citizens of the Colony, whereas the tribespeople were still considered foreigners. No concentrated effort was made to westernize and Christianize the tribespeople of the Colony and thus change the relationship.

But in the 1800s this did not bother the tribespeople in the Colony because they did not want to become western and therefore did not want western education. They had their own "schools" which prepared their children to become responsible adults according to their way of life: the Poro Society for boys and the Sande for girls. In time, however, the tribespeople began to see that a knowledge of basic English was necessary in order to live successfully in Freetown. By 1900 they wanted their children sent to school.

Meanwhile, in the middle 1800s, two American Missions arrived on the coast south of the Colony. The United Brethren in Christ Church (now Evangelical United Brethren) and the American Missionary Association, called the Mende Mission (which later was turned over to the Evangelical United Brethren), set up mission stations and schools around Shenge, a town on the peninsula forty-five miles south of Freetown, and around the waterways opposite Sherbro Island. They used the school approach, which had great prestige and, among the liberated Africans, great success. Each, at its main center, had a "Christian village" to keep the Christians from being contaminated by native life.

The missionaries taught in English, for it was partly known along the coast and was also a "Christian" language. Besides book knowledge the missionaries taught agriculture and technical skills such as carpentry and masonry. They hoped that by this education the boys would learn the European virtues of hard work and usefulness as well as Christianity. In common with the missionaries in the Colony, they concentrated on the children and youth, for they had no hope that adults could be changed.

The response of the Sherbro and Mende people to schools and Christianity was cautious and distrustful. If parents sent a child to school they did not think of it as giving him an education but as giving their child away. Not only did western education (and therefore Christianity) mean losing a potential farm worker, but it made a child unfit for manual labor. The child felt that manual labor and village life and even his nearest relatives were beneath him. He became detribalized and westernized. This was largely true when missionaries first began schools and remains largely true today. It is no wonder the tribespeople did not want to give up their children to school or to accept Christianity.

The reasons for the success of the school approach among the liberated Africans are the very reasons for its failure among the tribal people. The liberated Africans wanted to become western like the Settlers, and getting education and Christianity was the only way to achieve it. The tribal people, on the other hand, wanted to remain tribal, and education and Christianity detribalized. Moreover, the liberated Africans were saturated with the school approach, while the tribal people had only a few schools among their hundreds of villages.

Nevertheless, here and there, one by one, children were pulled out of their families and communities and educated. In some cases missionaries even paid the parents to send children to their school. This was to compensate the family for the loss of laborers as well as to establish contact in the town. As students gained sufficient education to become teachers they were sent to open other stations and start school-churches (every station had a school which was used as a church, or vice versa). Gradually more stations opened until, by the turn of the century, many of the main towns within twenty-five miles of the coast had schools. The tribal people resented this encroachment of the European culture upon their land and many reacted violently against it in the Hut Tax War, killing missionaries, native teachers, Creoles, white traders, and government police indiscriminately.

At the turn of the century the people of the Protectorate began to feel the need for education, as did the tribal people in the Colony. October 4, 1904, the Albert Academy, a boys' secondary school, was begun in Freetown by the Evangelical United Brethren Mission. Founded primarily to train boys from the Protectorate, it also admitted Creoles. In 1906 the government founded Bo School to provide western education for the sons and nominees of paramount chiefs; but education was still largely distrusted and many chiefs sent sons of domestic slaves rather than allow their own sons to be "contaminated." Many of these slaves later became chiefs, claiming as proof of their royalty the fact that they were sent to the school as chiefs' sons. In 1925 the government founded a boys' secondary school in Freetown, the Prince of Wales School.

As the years went by the country developed and opened up. The railroad and motor roads were built. Iron, gold, and diamonds were discovered. Cash crops such as ginger, cocoa, and coffee were grown. The suspicion of education and Christianity gradually decreased until now the whole country wants to become educated, but to remain African — westernized African. Moslems and animists alike are willing for their children to become Christians if only the government or Christian missions will start schools in their villages. This, plus competition between the Protestants and the Roman Catholics, has yielded a proliferation of schools throughout the country. In the process, the quality of teachers, both spiritual and educational, has greatly declined.

The educational statistics for 1963-64* were:

|  | No. of Schools | Enrollment | No. of Teachers |
|---|---|---|---|
| PRIMARY | 790 | 119,645 | 3331 |
| SECONDARY | 46 | 11,676 | 664 |

Less than half of those beginning primary school continue long enough to attain a functional literacy in English. Many drift into semi-literacy, too sophisticated to be of use on the farm and inadequate for clerical jobs.

Education meant a rise in the social scale for both the liberated Africans and those tribal people who went to school. Even as education eventually identified the liberated Africans with the Settlers and thus widened the social gap between them and the tribal people, so also education acculturated the educated tribesman to western ways and widened the social gap between him and his family and village.

Thus in Sierra Leone today there are three types of society. They do not mix socially and communication between them is formal.

First, *the Creole*. He is proud of his ancestry and feels himself superior to all other Sierra Leoneans. He has his own language, Krio (a special kind of pidgin English), but this is being replaced by ordinary pidgin. Many Creoles are uneducated and cannot speak or read English. Once the Creole was top man in Sierra Leone, with the exception of the white man. But just as he was about to drink the cup of success it was snatched from his hands by tribesmen. He and his brothers still, however, hold high hospital and other government positions. For many Creoles one mark of superiority is their Church, the Church of Sierra Leone (Anglican).

Second, *the educated tribesman*. He once copied the Creoles. Many of his fellows rejected their tribes and became Creoles. But now he is proud of his heritage (providing he does not get too close to it). He considers himself superior to the Creole. He and his brothers run the country and hold most of the salaried jobs. They, too, have churches, and theirs are less formal than those of the Creoles.

* Report of the Ministry of Education for 1965 (Sierra Leone Government).

Toward his uneducated tribesmen he has feelings of superiority — and embarrassment. He often feels he has more in common with the Creoles than with his uneducated brothers. He finds it hard to talk with them because he thinks differently and has acquired different values and interests. He cannot lower himself to soil his hands by doing manual labor, but neither can he escape from his family and his past. His relatives sacrificed and went hungry and ragged to educate him. Now they expect him to help them. His position as a salaried man means many expenses unknown to them. He is in debt. Yet they come and camp in his parlor, expecting a return for their investment.

Third, *the tribesman*. For centuries he has burned the bush and made farms. The village and farm are his life and sole interest. The spice of life, since wars have been prohibited, is attending court cases to hear woman palaver and bush palaver over boundaries. The day begins at dawn and ends at dusk, occasionally followed by dancing all night. Education is a nuisance, depriving him of farm help from his sons and daughters. He represents the vast majority of the people of Sierra Leone.

Each of the three types of society has many social levels and many nontypical individuals. Yet these descriptions are typical and show the social distance between the three types. This is important for church growth, for the Gospel tends to flow along specific lines of communication, the most important being the web of family relationships. Nevertheless, if there is a deep social gap between one group and another, even if they are of the same family, little communication of the Gospel takes place.

## MEANING FOR CHURCH GROWTH

Churches do not grow in a vacuum but among people — people who have fears and aspirations and are conditioned by centuries of tradition. These people have their accustomed ways of accepting changes. Thus the manner in which the Gospel is presented determines to a great extent how it will be received.

Also of great importance is the "ripeness," or receptivity, of the receiving people. People vary greatly in this respect.

Ripe fields can be harvested if right methods are used. The experienced harvester will recognize which peoples are ripe now and concentrate all his efforts toward harvesting the crop until the last head of rice is cut and stored in the barn. If the ripe area is too big for him to harvest alone he will call in extra help. He knows that rice is best for harvesting during a certain period and that if he delays too long it will spoil.

The analogy of the rice farm and harvest fits the missionary task — the Church's task — of bringing peoples to Christ. The term "people" refers to a tribe, or any ethnic group of people who have a sense of group oneness and social solidarity. The persons within it are a homogeneous unit. They think alike, have the same values, speak the same language, and feel themselves to be different from the other tribes or ethnic groups around them. Within a people are sections which are more ready to respond to the Gospel and accept Christ than others. For example, the Mende tribe is a people. All of its members speak the same language, are proud to be Mende, and feel themselves to be different from the other tribes around them. Within the Mende tribe are many sections, some of which are more ready to turn to Christ and become members of His Church than others.*

The missionary and national pastor must be sensitive to see which tribes are ready for harvest and which sections of a tribe are "ripest." When they discover such sections they must concentrate their efforts there and, if need be, send in more harvesters, even if it means that these other workers temporarily must leave their unreceptive areas. Only thus will the full harvest be gathered in. Even as ripe rice if left too long without being harvested will spoil, so also a "ripe" people have a period of receptivity. If they are not harvested when ready they will lose their desire to turn to Christ. The history of missions records many cases of people who were receptive to the Gospel but were not harvested, or were only partly harvested, so that later when harvesters came they were no longer receptive.

In Sierra Leone many factors affected the ripeness of its

* For an excellent and thorough discussion of homogeneous units or populations and their meaning for church growth, see chapter five of *Church Growth and Christian Mission* (McGavran 1965).

peoples. Some existed prior to the coming of the missionaries, others developed as the missionaries went about their work. In the light of this fact let us now see the meaning of the historical background to the growth of the Church in Sierra Leone.

1. The slave trade and tribal wars. Until the mid-1800s, slave trade and wars prevented the missionaries from entering the hinterland and confined them to the Colony and the coast. Since Christianity was identified with the white man and the slave trade, it was not seen as a revelation of the love of God. Nor did stopping the slave trade soften the people's attitudes, because many tribes were angered at the loss of their source of income.

2. The number of tribes and languages. This has often been given as an excuse for not learning the vernacular languages. Historians have claimed there were too many to learn. This was true in the Colony when large numbers of liberated Africans arrived, although some missionaries tried to learn the languages of the larger groups. But English triumphed in the Colony, making knowledge of the vernaculars unnecessary. In the Protectorate English did not triumph, but most of the missionaries found enough English-speaking natives to enable them to get by without learning the vernaculars. This definitely hindered the acceptance of the Gospel and prevented the identification of the Good News with the tribal way of life.

3. The "depravity" of the tribal people and their way of life. The missionaries, considering the whole native culture to be evil, did not believe it possible for a native to become Christian and continue his former way of life. They had confused western civilization with Christianity and considered it just as important to civilize the people as to Christianize them. Indeed, they thought the natives could not be Christianized unless they were first civilized. Thus, although the missionaries preached to the adults, they did not expect many to respond, but pinned their hopes upon the children and youth. Because Christianity was identified with civilization and education, the tribesmen did not want any of it.

4. The Settlers. The Settlers were Christians but had no desire to win the tribal people. They had been delivered to a hostile land, and all their energies were directed toward secur-

ing a stable colony. The natives were not looked upon as subjects for conversion but as threats to the existence of the Colony. The coming of the liberated Africans also threatened the Settlers' "superior" way of life, so the Settlers kept aloof.

5. The liberated Africans. They were "ripe" for the Gospel. Although their motives for becoming Christian were largely based upon their desire to achieve the prestige of the Settlers, there can be no doubt that they became Christian. They identified themselves with the Settlers and eventually were assimilated as Creoles, thus becoming socially separated from the tribal people, with no bridge for the communication of the Gospel.

(Although the liberated Africans did not convey the Gospel to the tribal people of Sierra Leone, many of them returned to their homelands and were instrumental in opening their tribes for the Gospel and missionary societies. Samuel Crowther, Bishop of Nigeria, was one of them. But their stories belong to the church growth histories of their respective lands.)

6. The Creoles. The Creole today still feels superior and hostile toward the "natives," both educated and uneducated. His attitude toward them prevents identification and evangelism.

7. The effect of education upon the tribesmen. The government, Churches, and Missions have been doing their best to provide the needed education for today and tomorrow in Sierra Leone. But such education detribalizes and tends to hinder evangelism — a side effect that cannot be avoided. The great majority of the people are not literate, nor will they be literate within their lifetime, or their children's lifetime, or that of their children's children, unless the present situation greatly improves. If the Church is to win the peoples of Sierra Leone for Christ and plant churches throughout the land, she must communicate the Good News to the people in a way that will be meaningful to their way of life.

A few educated tribesmen certainly have won villagers to Christ. In fact, what success there has been among the tribes is due mainly to them. They have partially succeeded where the Creoles have failed. Yet, this is exceptional. Usually, the higher their education, the more difficult it is for them to mix socially with the villagers and evangelize them.

8. Sierra Leone development and progress. The people of Sierra Leone now see and desire the advantages of progress. When people are ready for social change, that is the easiest time for religious change. Peoples in Sierra Leone are ripe for harvesting into the Kingdom of God, some of them more so than others. As those who are the most ready are converted and brought into active service in numerous churches, others will more quickly become ready.

However, with a few exceptions, *the ripe peoples in Sierra Leone are not being harvested!* How can they be brought to Christ? Their social structure and religion will affect the way in which they respond to the Gospel. To that we now turn.

# CHAPTER 3

# TRIBAL RELIGION AND SOCIAL STRUCTURE

## ANIMISM

Animism, the original religion of Sierra Leone, is still predominant and is basically the same among the various tribes. Animists do not worship weekly or regularly as do Christians and Muslims. Rather, their worship is personal, familial, and communal for specific occasions. The presuppositions of animism pervade the whole life of the people, even after they have become Muslim or Christian, and are an integrating part of the people's culture. Animism in Sierra Leone, particularly among the Mende, can be grouped into six categories: Supreme God, nature spirits, ancestral spirits, mischievous spirits, spirits of the secret societies, and an impersonal power.*

The Supreme God created the world and everything in it, including the spirits and a certain impersonal power which pervades the whole world. The power or influence shows itself in different ways and on certain occasions in both humans and animals, and in natural phenomena such as lightning, mountains, and waterfalls. The people believe that ages ago God lived closer to man but that now he lives far away in the sky. Although he has power over everything, he has delegated power to the spirits, and it is with them that the people have most to deal. The people call themselves the children of God, or the Supreme Being, and believe him to be good. However, he is thought of as Chief rather than as Father. Although God's name is used directly in blessings and curses and in emergencies, people usually approach him through interme-

* For the discussion of animism among the Mende I am indebted to K. L. Little, *The Mende of Sierra Leone* (1951).

diaries (the most common ones being ancestral spirits), as befits a great Chief.

The nature spirits, although everywhere, are usually associated with natural phenomena such as rivers, the bush and unusual trees, rocks, or waterfalls. Because these spirits have tastes and emotions similar to humans, people come to them for help. These spirits, however, are not very reliable, and one must be cautious lest one become possessed.

The ancestral spirits are the most helpful of all the spirits, as they live among the living and are regarded as part of the family. Each extended family has its own cult to get protection, health, and wealth from its ancestors. The head of the family or its oldest member is usually the one to perform ceremonies to secure help from the ancestors. The people believe the ancestors have power to help them directly, but sometimes they ask the ancestors to carry the prayers to God.

The mischievous spirits are the ones held responsible for minor misfortunes, sickness, and accidents. They have no specific names as do the ancestral and nature spirits. Occasionally people make small offerings to them or scatter a "medicine" around the farms and gardens to prevent these spirits from doing harm.

The spirits of the secret societies, called devils, are involved in all society activities. They give the societies power and enforce their rules. For example, members will perform all rituals asked of them by the society superior and will not tell society secrets to nonmembers for fear of what the devils (not to mention other society members) will do to them.

*Hale* is the Mende word for the impersonal force which pervades the world. This is the force (usually translated as "medicine") which operates "medicines," charms, tabus, omens, and curses and underlies many practices of the tribes of Sierra Leone, including secret societies, to which the word *hale* also refers. This force is amoral and can be used for good or evil. The word, among the Mende, also refers to any object or tool used to gain specific ends by supernatural means.

For example, babies, being the most susceptible to harm, receive the most protection from "medicine." They are heavily weighted down with pouches, teeth, and other objects tied around their necks, wrists, loins, and ankles. The Mende, however, make a distinction between a knotted string with specially prepared objects tied to it which is made by special men to keep away witches and sickness, and another kind of string, metal bracelet, or anklet which is made by anyone to keep snakes from biting or minor misfortunes from occurring. Only the former is referred to as *hale*.

Other uses of "medicine" are swearing and cursing. If a man has a renowned "medicine," people from scores of miles away will come to swear on it so that some good may come to them or some evil will come to their enemies. In court certain "medicines" are used to swear on so that the one testifying will be afraid to lie. On fruit trees "medicines" will be tied to prevent stealing. Passers-by will fear to steal fruit lest the "medicine" follow and harm them.

Witchcraft is in the category of the impersonal force. The people believe that witches cause the death of most babies. Witches (male or female) have witch-spirits within them. The witch can control his witch-spirit and send it out to "eat" people, usually children. Witch-finders of renown are often called to come and help in time of sickness or if many babies die in a short period of time. The unpopular person is often accused by the witch-finder of being a witch.

Life is filled with uncertainties and dangers. The animist, in his belief in spirits and "medicine," feels he knows why misfortune comes and how to cope with it or prevent it. Help is forthcoming from spirits and "medicine." All else failing, he looks to the Supreme God who, although far away and not directly concerned in man's affairs, has the most power and will give help in time of need.

*Meaning for Church Growth*

The missionary and national pastor seeking to win these people for Christ must ask, What meaning has this system of belief for church growth? How can such people be led to faith in Christ and active service in His Church? What beliefs will they have when they become Christian? It is not within the scope of this book to answer these questions exhaustively, but some basic principles can be cited.

First, Christianity has points of contact with the animism of these people. The most obvious are: the belief in the benevolence of God and the awareness of spirit power. The first principle, then, is that the Christian worker, in his teaching, can assume a common foundation.

Second, Christ has shown that God is not far off, but near. His power is greater than all the spirits around, so people need fear them no more, nor need they seek succor from any spirit or power other than God. When a person sins, it is God who is offended, so it is toward Him that sinners should be penitent and from Him that they receive forgiveness.

Third, the people's awareness of the spirit world enables them to be more easily aware of the presence of God. The degree to which education has caused loss of belief in the spirit world is in many cases the degree to which sensitivity toward the Spirit of God has been lost. Jacob Loewen (1964 11:97-104), missionary to the animistic Choco Indians of Latin America, shows this quite clearly in his article, "The Choco and Their Spirit World." The belief in spirits should not be dismissed out of hand. Rather, this belief should be used to achieve a strong sense of the presence and power of the true God.

Fourth, the greatest obstacle to thorough conversion and strong Christian faith is this same belief in spirits and particularly the belief in the efficacy of "medicine." Many converts do not transfer faith completely from these to God, but continue to participate in sacrifices at the burial of a relative or in seeking help from the ancestral spirits. Many still accept charms from their grandmothers to tie on their babies. What is needed is a radical break from and rejection of these things. This means a powerful meeting with God in which each convert rejects the material symbol of the pagan power in which he has hitherto believed. This is essential. Such a rejection would be strengthened by a people movement in which a sufficient number are won in a short enough period of time that family pressure to participate in the old ways is removed.

## ISLAM

John Mendelson, in *God, Allah and Juju: Religion in Africa Today,* writes:

Tiny Sierra Leone numbers 588,000 Moslems among its

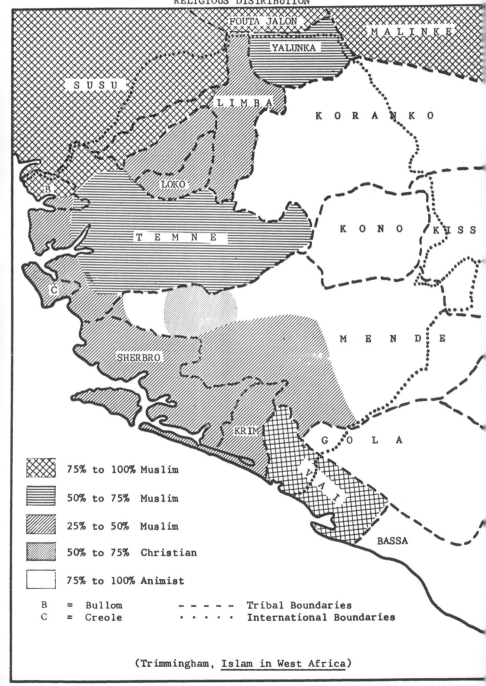

RELIGIOUS DISTRIBUTION

FOUTA JALON

MALINKE

YALUNKA

SUSU

KORANKO

LIMBA

LOKO

KONO    KISS

TEMNE

B

C

MENDE

SHERBRO

KRIM    GOLA

VAI

BASSA

⊠⊠ 75% to 100% Muslim

≡ 50% to 75% Muslim

⫽ 25% to 50% Muslim

▒ 50% to 75% Christian

☐ 75% to 100% Animist

B  =  Bullom       – – – – –  Tribal Boundaries
C  =  Creole       · · · · ·  International Boundaries

(Trimmingham, Islam in West Africa)

2,350,000 people, and 70,000 Christians. Most of the rest maintain their old customs and beliefs. Typical of West Africa in general, one is likely to find a miscellany of religions in a single family or village. The atmosphere is tolerant, and religious affiliation is not a focus for strong feelings (1962).

J. Spencer Trimmingham, in *Islam in West Africa,* sees Sierra Leone as a picture of religious confusion. The map on page 46 reveals this. In commenting on the catholicity of Muslim chiefs he says:

> They keep up the ancestral cult and the *poro* for they are part of the body of custom they have to maintain, they support Islam to the extent of becoming adherents, and they encourage Christian missions out of appreciation of their work in education and social welfare, attending church services at festivals as they also honour Islamic festivals. The three religions each fulfill a social function, and since adherents of all are found in each chieftancy, all are accorded recognition. But the position is not stable. Islam, as religion of the rulers that anyone can join regardless of status or class, naturally tends to dominate. Although villagers may be uninterested in Islam the village chief may think it wise to profess it (1959).

Islam had become firmly established in the Sudan north of Sierra Leone near the Sahara by the end of the eleventh century. Since then it has spread as far as the coast of Sierra Leone. The coastal and forest areas to the south and east are not yet under the influence of Islam.

In a real sense, Sierra Leone represents the transition from animism to Islam. Except for the Susu and Yalunka, Sierra Leone was animist when the Nova Scotians were settled to form the Colony, although a few chiefdoms in Limbaland and Lokoland and one in Temneland were ruled by Madinka or Fula Muslim chiefs. Most of the Muslims lived as traders in various centers, but kept to themselves in separate communities at the edge of the villages and at first had little effect upon the life of the people. The people valued their trading services, and more especially their religious influence and ability to make powerful "medicine." The Muslim community grew mostly by the increase in their own families, and to only a small extent by intermarriage with local women.

By the early 1900s Muslims had much influence with the chiefs, many of whom were already Muslim. Whereas earlier the chiefs had welcomed missionaries to come and preach in the main towns near the coast, now they were hostile. Soon after a school was opened in Konoland in 1910, the Muslims stirred up the chiefs, and there was opposition. But five years later disputes within the Muslim community broke the solid opposition, and since then there has been no open Muslim opposition in Konoland. Elsewhere in Sierra Leone the opposition to Christianity also began to subside until there came to be a tripartite coexistence: animist, Muslim, and Christian. Coexistence, however, did not mean equality. The animists greatly outnumbered the others, the tiny fringe of Christians in some larger towns were the educated, and in many places the Muslims were in political control.

This century the tribes of Sierra Leone are experiencing people movements to Islam. (See religious distribution map on p. 46.) First, the whole Vai tribe became Muslim. Later, the Temne, Loko, and Limba began moving into Islam. These people movements are still active, with half the Temne and a large segment of the Limba almost solidly Muslim. Recently the Mende have begun to move into Islam, more rapidly near the coast, but also in the rest of Mendeland.

Some of the many reasons for this spread of Islam are: (1) Islam has had nine centuries to adapt itself to West African culture. The type of Islam spreading in Sierra Leone, except for its use of Arabic, is thoroughly West African. (2) The stigma of being a religion of slave raiders and conquerors is long a thing of the past. (3) Much of Islamic thought has diffused into the indigenous animistic thought, thus bringing the two religions closer together. (4) Islam has prestige by possessing chiefdom political power. (5) Islam permits polygamy. (6) Muslims have greater control over their women, who are more faithful and are punished for adultery. (7) Islam today among the educated and secularized has the prestige of being "the religion of the Blacks," whereas Christianity has the stigma of being "the religion of the Whites." The two religions are frequently characterized in these terms by Muslim advocates.

The type of Islam the people are accepting is animistic,

with an overlay of Muslim belief and practice. All Muslims say the creed, "There is no God but God, and Mohammed is his prophet." The rich make pilgrimages to Mecca and thereby become holy and receive the title of "Alhaja," by which they must be called thereafter. The devout observe the fast of Ramadan with its feasting after dark. All share in the festivities at the close of the Ramadan fast, and the animists and Christians help them celebrate. Many set aside a tithe of their produce for use in feeding the poor and guests who come to them.

Devout Muslim men do not participate in secret societies, but their women join Sande. The very devout will pray the required five times a day. The less devout will pray two or three times a day — once in the morning and twice in the evening. Many Muslims do not pray at all, yet they hold to their creed. The prayers are chanted responsively in Arabic (which is spoken without understanding by most of the participants), and accompanied by kneeling, prostrations, and hand movements. Most Muslim communities of any size have one or more priests called "Alfas" who conduct the prayers in the mosques. They can read Arabic, but only a few of them can understand what they read. Although the chanted prayers are in Arabic, opportunity is given for members of the congregation to utter personal petitions. Throughout the land small groups of boys in little Koranic "schools" are learning to chant the Arabic Koran, but without comprehension. The Muslim priests do not receive salaries. Their food is supplied by the chiefs, and they make money by practicing "medicine."

The above describes the distinctive Muslim character of Islam in Sierra Leone. The following describes its animistic elements. The first Muslims in Mendeland were called *morimen* because they were powerful in the use of "medicine." The words of the Koran (in Arabic) are believed to have power. When written on paper and enclosed in pouches, they make excellent charms. Almost all Muslims wear them, although they are most noticeable on children. These words written over the doors protect houses. When written on boards and placed in farms or hung from trees, they prevent stealing. Chiefs commonly use them to divine the future. They are the most potent of oaths to force people to tell the truth. In all these cases, it is the mori-man who manipulates the power in the Koran to achieve these ends. The term mori-man still is used among the Mende to refer to a Muslim "medical" practitioner; however, the term has come to be the common word for Muslim.

The most obvious effects of Islamic thought and practice upon its animistic counterparts are: (1) a more definite concept of the sky god as the Supreme Being, (2) a stronger belief in a future Day of Judgment, (3) a stronger idea of fatalism, (4) the introduction of many new words (among the Mende) such as *jumbui* (to sin) and *seli* (to pray), and (5) burial rites.

The Ahmadiyah movement has come into Sierra Leone with missionaries from Pakistan. Its aim is to purify West African Islam, as well as to win all the people. One of the methods is the school approach, and it is militantly anti-Christian. However, its success so far in Sierra Leone is small.

## Meaning for Church Growth

Although the readiness of Sierra Leoneans for change makes them ripe for accepting the Gospel, it also makes them ripe for accepting Islam. The Islam they accept may be a very corrupt form and unrecognizable to "pure" Muslims elsewhere. It may be Islamized paganism and many of its followers may be nominal, but it is Islam — and its followers feel themselves to be incorporated into its vast brotherhood. From the point of view of church growth, Islam makes them much more resistant to the Gospel. It is therefore imperative that the Churches of Jesus Christ concentrate on winning the peoples of Sierra Leone for Christ and planting churches among them. To do this will require drastic modification of present methods and strategy for harvesting whole peoples into the Kingdom of God.

## SOCIAL STRUCTURE

The social structure of a people is an important factor in determining how innovations, such as new religions, are accepted. In western society each person is encouraged to make decisions on his own without consulting others. This cultural trait is strengthened through the breakdown of the wider family into independent nuclear units and through great mobility. The evangelism which works best in this kind of social structure is one which seeks individual conversions.

But western social structure with its fragmented society is unique among the societies of the world. The social structure of most peoples, including the tribes of Sierra Leone, has solidarity and interdependence. Decisions are not usually made without consulting others. Evangelism in societies of this kind, to be effective, must aim at winning social units by encouraging internal discussion and informal vote-taking until these units are won for Christ.

*Decision-making Bodies*

The basic social unit* in tribal Sierra Leone is the household, which often contains three generations. Its number of members varies greatly, but a large-sized household may consist of one or two older men and their wives, some or all of their sons and daughters, husbands and wives of the latter, and a number of grandchildren. Such a household may also contain additional members such as more distant relatives (either from the husbands' or the wives' side), as well as one or more dependents of the head of the household who are unrelated to the rest of the group. A small-sized household, on the other hand, may consist only of a man and his wife or wives and their children, and one or two close relatives, such as his mother or sister. If a stranger, either of the same tribe or of another tribe, wishes to live in a town, he is lodged as the guest of one of the households and as long as he stays there is considered a member of it. Almost all decisions are made within the household. Major decisions, such as arranging inheritance, would be made within the whole extended family.**

* This section refers mainly to the Mende and Kono. However, their social structures are typical of most tribes in Sierra Leone.
** An extended family may be identical with the household in the cases of larger households, but usually it would involve more than one household. The extended family of the Mende includes the oldest living male, his brothers, his and their wives, and all male and unmarried female descendants, excluding the children of women who have married into other families.
The Kono extended family is larger in that it is a joint family but, like the Mende, is patrilocal, i.e., upon marriage the wife leaves her

The dwellings of a household are usually clustered in compact family compounds. A small village may have only one household. A larger town may have as many as five or six households. The settlement pattern consists of a large central town with outlying villages which usually have family houses in the central town. In heavily populated areas the villages may be only one-half mile to two miles apart. In less populated areas they may be three to six miles apart. In the grasslands in the north, towns may be ten to fifteen miles apart without any intervening villages.

The tribes are organized under paramount chiefs over small districts from five to twenty-five miles square called chiefdoms, and these are subdivided into sections, each with a section chief. The section in turn comprises towns or villages, each having its town chief and council of elders. Among the Mende the descendants of the original settlers are the ruling families and the land owners. They are the ones eligible to become section or paramount chiefs. In a ritual sense, a chief is owner of everything under his authority, including people.

Secret societies are an important part of the people's life. They are no longer secret because descriptions of them have been written by anthropologists and are available in public libraries. The predominant societies are the Poro for males and the Sande for females. Their chief function is to prepare adolescents for adult life. One of the rites for the initiates, in common with most West African secret societies, is circumcision for the boys and clitoridectomy for the girls. These societies also exercise a controlling influence in politics. The uprising in 1898 (the Hut Tax War) was planned in the Poro and kept secret from all outsiders.

### Meaning for Church Growth

A people movement in a tightly knit clan works in the following way. Before a member of the clan can change his religion, if he wishes to remain a part of the clan and avoid ostracism, he must consult with the other members. He will

home to live with her husband and his family, and patrilineal, i.e., inheritance is reckoned through the male line. Also, the Kono have clans, and their marriage pattern is exogamous, i.e., all marriages must be outside the clan.

avoid formally changing his religion, e.g., by accepting baptism, until a sufficient number of other members also desire to change. This will require a period of time during which discussion and informal vote-taking will occur. At first the clan may be against the change. But gradually, one by one, members may change their minds. The occasional visits of the itinerating evangelist, or the influence of a nearby group of Christians, may help them to make this decision. Finally enough persons are convinced so that when the matter is discussed at a clan meeting, the whole clan (or extended family), or most of it, turns to Christ.

The advantage of such a movement is that the group comes in with its own leaders, with its own organizational structure, and with its own effective system of discipline. The members do not need to be provided with leaders because they have their own; the Church and Mission need only train the natural leaders. The members do not need to be provided with a foreign form of organization to order church life because they have their own. As far as form is concerned, the Church and Mission need only teach them • the functions, rituals, and activities necessary to carry on church life and worship. The members do not need to be given methods of discipline because they have their own. The Church and Mission need only bring them to the experience of grace and teach them the principles of Christian living based on love and how to apply them to local conditions.

Tightly knit social segments among the Fijians, the Batak of Northern Sumatra, the Karens of Burma, the Papuans of New Guinea, and many others have moved into the Church in this way. Where the movement was followed up through training the natural leaders, the resulting churches became strong and vigorous, fully self-supporting, self-governing, self-propagating, and, to a large extent, self-lifting (that is, they improved their material environment with their own resources). Where natural leaders were not trained, or were trained inadequately, many members lapsed back into their former ways or neopaganism.

The large homogeneous units in Sierra Leone are not so tightly knit, perhaps because of western influence. The large degree of permissiveness with respect to religion mentioned earlier is misleading. Large social units such as the clan or chiefdom are permissive, but extended families, and especially households, exert much more control. In some cases the family desired knowledge of, and influence in, all the religions and sent sons for training to each — Protestant, Roman Catholic, and Muslim. The cases of children being sent to Christian operated schools is another indication of permissiveness.

But most families are concerned that all their members adhere to the same religion. As we shall see later, conversion among the nonliterates tends to follow family lines. Thus, to achieve greater church growth, concentration of evangelism should be aimed at the whole family rather than at one individual within the family. Moreover, non-Christian households which are related to Christian households located in different areas should be sought out and made objects of special evangelistic effort. Their relationship to the Christian households provides bridges* over which Christianity can enter their households and villages.

The first meaning for church growth, then, is that the family structure can be used as a vehicle for discipling peoples and bringing them into responsible membership in Christ's Church.

The second meaning has to do with leadership. Large, tightly knit social units have leaders who naturally lead their people as they form into churches. The same is true of households, extended families, villages, and towns. These leaders are mature married men and women accustomed to making decisions and seeing that they are carried out. As households, families, and large segments of villages and towns turn to Christ, the leadership ability of these men and women ought to be utilized. They are gifts of God. To send them unmarried, immature, detribalized young men to lead them and be their pastors is a poor way to build strong Christians and strong churches. Perhaps educated youth are needed among literate and semi-literate transient town people, but most of them are ineffective among nonliterate village people whose life is the soil.

This applies to situations where many people are coming

---

* See Donald McGavran's excellent discussion of how blood relationships provide bridges for the Gospel to move from one group of people to another in *The Bridges of God* (1955).

to Christ within a limited time and area, that is, people movements. These statements do not apply to the school approach
of one-by-one conversions, with one or two Christians in one
village and a handful in another and a core of teachers and
pupils at the central station. The school approach is not winning the peoples of Sierra Leone to Christ; the people movement approach will. The problem of how the natural leaders
within the people movements can be trained to be effective
church leaders will be discussed later.

*Marriage Patterns*

In tribal Sierra Leone, as in all of tribal Africa, polygamy
is regarded as the ideal marriage pattern. Two aspects of this
in the tribes of Sierra Leone are bride price, often coupled
with premarital bride service, and the marriage of widows to
their brothers-in-law. Additional wives are important and
desired because (1) they increase the social prestige of the
husband and, to some extent, that of his present wife or wives;
(2) they are a symbol of wealth; (3) they enable large farms to
be worked; (4) they provide more hands to gather food and
do household chores, and thus provide more freedom for
the wives; (5) they free one of the wives to do trading and
thus bring in extra money; (6) they permit the husband to have
marital intercourse when one of the wives is pregnant, nursing,
sick, or otherwise unavailable, and (7) they provide the family
with more children.

Polygamy is intricately woven into the social fabric of the
people. It is desired by both men and women, and they see
nothing basically wrong with the system. Bride price is regarded
as appreciation to the girl's parents for bringing the girl up and
caring for her. They can always point to at least one polygamous household in the village which runs smoothly and without internal strife, and this confirms the ideal. Marriage is
regarded primarily as an alliance between two kinship groups
and only in a secondary aspect as a union between two individual persons. This statement can easily be pressed too far,
but it does show that the indigenous institution of marriage can
be understood only if it is viewed as an integral part of the
kinship system as a whole and as a matter of economics.
Marriage therefore is a transaction giving rise to reciprocal

rights and obligations between two groups of kinsmen, and binding those groups together in a relationship which remains effective beyond the lifetime of the original individual spouses. We saw earlier how this relationship can act as a bridge to communicate the Gospel from one extended family to another.

The foregoing is the positive side of the system of polygamy. We now turn to the negative side. First, and the thing most fundamentally wrong with polygamy, is the attitude toward women. In a system of marriage based on an economy in which the male plays the dominating role, women are regarded as economic assets, laborers, and child producers rather than as persons. However, this is not always true, for many men have respect and affection for women and in not a few cases women have even achieved political power.

In days past the happiness of the girl was not considered when arranging for marriages. Fathers sometimes pledged their infant females to friends who were middle-aged or even senile. Today, although this still goes on, girls are permitted to say yes or no after they have graduated from Sande. However, when the time comes, family pressure often ensures an affirmative answer.

Second, there are not enough girls to achieve the ideal. The ratio of males to females, according to the 1963 census, is roughly one to one. Men who are monogamous are so not by choice but by circumstance, and thousands are single. Among the Kono one of the solutions for the single man is to attach himself to a polygamous household and in return for labor, receive food, enough clothing to keep covered, a place to sleep, and sexual privileges with one of the wives. Many a tribesman who remains single continues to work on his father's farm and becomes a lover of a dissatisfied wife. Sometimes such a relationship results in the wife leaving her husband and eloping with her lover. Unmarried school teachers and even village evangelists have been known to have "friendships"* with married women.

---

* "Friendship" indicates a temporary relationship involving sexual contacts. "Friends" may either live together or meet only occasionally. If they live together for longer than a month, they are referred to as married, but nothing binds the relationship and it can, and usually does, end at any time.

Third, lack of wealth is another reason for the difficulty in getting a wife. Many men do not have the resources to pay a bride price. Consequently, marriages are undertaken after a series of friendships. These friendships may have begun during initiation days.

Many more unfortunate aspects of the polygamous system could be presented. Jealousy, envy, wife neglect, adultery, and witch accusation are the most common. However, such evils are not peculiar to polygamous households; they are common to sinful man, regardless of marriage pattern.

Both positive and negative aspects show the economic nature of the problem and why polygamy, if desirable from the tribal point of view, is undesirable from the standpoint of Christian ethics.

Polygamy has often been named the number one reason for slow church growth in West Africa. Whether or not this is so, the Church's law requiring monogamy before a person may be baptized or received into full membership has been a deterrent to the spread of Christianity. No less a person than Bishop Newbigin concurs in this. The law ought to be reconsidered for two reasons.

First, the law prohibiting polygamy was promulgated without a clear understanding of the complexity of the polygamous system. Christian leaders have often condemned the system out of hand without any attempt to understand it. William D. Reyburn has written an excellent presentation titled, "Polygamy, Economy, and Christianity in the Eastern Cameroun." In his editorial introduction to the article he says:

> Motivations for polygamy are a complex set of cultural factors which have not and will not be readily changed. Christianity in its total condemnation of polygamy has failed to discriminate between things which are totally different. The emphasis upon monogamy has often led Africans into a false picture of the monogamous union and a resultant reaction to it. While there are certain immediate and practical steps Christian churches can take concerning polygamy, *the church is neither equipped nor is it operating in the real sphere of its message by following these superficial approaches to the problem.* The Christian church, particularly Protestant, makes its fatal mistake in attempting to operate with neither a formulated missionary science nor

an articulate missionary theology. From the side of missionary science we must learn that the case involved in this area is *primarily economic and not primarily isolated polygamy*. From the side of missionary theology we need to take the findings of such information and in true Christian identification with the human being involved move with our theology to his inner longings and *WITH HIM* communicate a gospel that speaks to the roots of his real need and show him that Christ is the ultimate answer to the *POWER* problem of his heart. When this has been done the transformed individual displays a transformation of symbols in his new relation to the power of the gospel and his regenerate life (1962; italics mine).

In developing these ideas he points out that there are two factors which would automatically lead toward monogamy: (1) male and female equality of rights, with mutual respect, and (2) the existence of a complex class system in which hired laborers are available. The second factor is a problem of cultural change which will eventually come. The Church can do little about this except to aid progress through education.

But as for the first factor, the Church should do a great deal. The emphasis should not be "no polygamy — monogamy only," but rather should be on teaching Christian village men to think of their wives as partners in a permanent marriage concerned for the welfare of their families. This would help turn their eyes from the economic aspect of marriage to the personal. With respect to the power problem spoken of in the introduction to his article, Reyburn sees polygamy with its children, crops, gardens, and wives as signs of the power traditional Africans seek to possess. The search for this kind of power and its symbols must be transformed and directed toward a search for the power of the Gospel and its symbols of the Church with its corporate worship and sacraments.

Second, the law requiring monogamy before a person may be baptized, hold office in the Church, or commune implies that abstention from polygamy is a necessary evidence of conversion. But is this Christian? Is it true to the Gospel and the New Testament? Roland Allen, in his "St. Paul and the Judaizers," points out that missionary societies (and national church leaders who follow the patterns they set) fail to see that their insistence on acceptance of certain moral laws before baptism and admission into the church is the same insistence that the Judaizers made with respect to admitting the Gentiles into the Church. The Judaizers, insisting that circumcision and obedience to the Jewish law with its high moral code be a prerequisite to baptism, felt they were following the will of God. Western Christians' and Creoles' insistence upon the law of monogamy as a prerequisite to baptism and communion is of the same sort. But the Gospel is that salvation is through faith (Ephesians 2:8, 9).

In his book, *The Spontaneous Expansion of the Church,* Roland Allen notes:

> There are two ways of maintaining a standard of morals. We may keep the ideal presented to us in Christ ever before ourselves and our converts, and seek ourselves, and teach them, to follow it, or we may define a standard and treat that definition as a law which must not be departed from. In the first case we set before our converts an infinite advance, in the second a finite rule. In the first case we must trust in the Spirit to lead them towards that divine standard of morality, in the second we can trust in our powers of control and direction. ... In the first case we accept a divine standard, both for ourselves and for our converts; in the second we present what seems to us to be a proper standard, a standard which is more or less Christian, as the case may be, a standard which appears to us Christian, but is something short of the standard of Christ (1960).

He then shows how arbitrary church laws are, and that "they are not always in themselves unquestionably clear expressions of divine law about which no Christian can have any doubt."

Monogamy is such a law; and further, it has led to some absurdities. Although monogamy as an official rule for baptism is uniform in theory for all Churches, it is not uniform in practice. This may be because some recognize the nonspiritual character of the law. In one outstation church interviewed, when asked how many men had more than one wife, the supervising minister (a teacher-agent was in charge) requested to be excused from answering. He did not want to know who were polygamous, because he felt that if he knew, he would have to discipline. He was obliged to obey the law and enforce it, but felt it ought not to be enforced.

The Christian polygamist sees nothing morally wrong with polygamy as such, even as the Christian smoker sees nothing wrong with smoking, or as the Christian drinker sees nothing wrong with moderate drinking, or as the Christian driver sees nothing wrong with exceeding the speed limit a little, or as many Christians see nothing wrong with divorce and remarriage under certain circumstances.

True, such activities are not God's best plan of living for His children, but change in such activities must arise from a change within, from the prompting and conviction of the Holy Spirit, not from law. A person can be a devout and faithful Christian without obeying any of these laws — so long as in his heart he is not convinced of the spiritual necessity of obeying them.

To illustrate that the Christian polygamist sees nothing wrong with polygamy as such I will cite some instances. In one village, in which half (about forty) of the population, including the chief, had decided to follow Christ and were desiring to be baptized, I questioned the candidates for baptism. The people had been informed of the moral requirements of the Church, particularly concerning monogamy. All the people said they believed Christ died for them and they wanted to leave their old ways and follow Christ. The chief also said he had only one wife, but when the third woman bearing his name was questioned, he admitted he had three. He felt the need of baptism but, because he could not send his wives away, he lied.

In another village, in answer to the question regarding number of wives, a candidate with two wives said he had only one. He admitted he was living with a second woman but claimed that she was not his wife and that from now on he would not live with her. In truth he was married to her and had no intention of sending her away. Because of the Church's law he was willing to admit adultery and to lie in order to be baptized.

These cases illustrate the problems that can result when the Church insists upon obedience to law before a person can be considered a Christian, even as the Judaizers did in Paul's day. They show that the Church is demanding that a believer become westernized before he can become a Christian.

In one parish of thousands of Christians, most of them unbaptized, the ordained minister enforces the law of monogamy. No one will be baptized who is polygamous, nor will anyone be admitted to communion who has taken a second wife after baptism. But this does not mean that the Christians see the necessity of monogamy; rather, it means that the majority of Christians see the impossibility of baptism. When questioned about baptism they equated it with monogamy. They thought of baptism as a symbol of having only one wife, a higher level of Christianity that they did not expect to achieve until they were old. The standard by which Christians in the villages evaluated each other was based on church attendance and the quality of lives they led. They made no distinction between those baptized and those not; between those polygamous and those not.

The law of monogamy has been emphasized to such an extent that Christians see only the law and not the spiritual principle behind it. The principle and guide for living that underlies the law (and all laws) is love in personal relationships. The teachings that ought to be emphasized are (1) how husbands and wives should treat each other, (2) how parents ought to treat their children, and (3) how a Christian home ought to be established. If *these* are emphasized, the Spirit of God will have greater opportunity to convince the believers that such relationships can best be achieved through monogamous unions.

Joseph Wold in *God's Impatience in Liberia* (1968) says, "On some mission fields polygamy has been blown up all out of proportion to its true significance. This is the case in Liberia. The Old Testament accepted polygamy but forbade adultery."

This is also the case in Sierra Leone. Polygamy as a system of marriage is on its way out; not because of the Church, but because of the change in economics. It behooves the Church not to make an issue of a dying system. Wisely most of the Churches have left the question of secret societies alone, knowing they will change for the better. Certainly in some areas where the Church is strong, societies have less power than they once had. The same hands-off policy should apply to polygamy.

Lesslie Newbigin, in his book *Honest Religion for Secular Man,* looks at polygamy and says,

> ... in the history of missions in Africa it has been more or less taken for granted that the abandonment of polygamy is always and at all times an essential mark of conversion. There are some, of whom I am one, who believe this is both wrong on theological grounds and disastrous in missionary practice. I do not doubt for a moment that monogamy is God's will for the human family. But I also have no doubt that a man married in accordance with traditional practice and in good faith to several wives can be truly converted and enter into a personal knowledge of God through Jesus Christ in the fellowship of God's people, and that it is through that knowledge that he can learn how to order his family life. I am sure, incidentally, that this ordering cannot rightly include the act of abandoning women who have been married to him in honesty and good faith according to the custom and conscience of the society in which they have lived. In other words, I deny an absolute identification of conversion with a particular ethical decision in the matter of polygamy (1966: 73-74).

## DIAMOND MINING

The discussion of social structure would not be complete without mentioning the emergence of a fourth stratum of society. This is a transient population of nonliterate and semi-literate young men (and the women who follow them) who want to escape the tedium of farm and village life and earn money. Their *lingua franca* is pidgin English. The work most of them seek is diamond mining. Diamonds in Sierra Leone are alluvial and obtained from open pits.

Many of the men become employees of diamond mining companies and live more or less stable lives in the housing provided for them. But job openings are limited. Many more flock to the areas where the latest rumors say there are many diamonds, and attach themselves to diamond mining license holders. Diamond mining towns are mushrooming all along the upper Sewa River and in Konoland. Their populations fluctuate with the tide of rumors. Some diggers (the local term used for this kind of diamond miner) become fairly permanent residents of these towns and send for their wives, or find local women to marry. But most of them remain transient. Although the overall ratio of men to women in Sierra Leone is one to one, the diamond mining areas have a much higher ratio, which leaves the farm towns and villages with a slightly higher ratio of women to men.

License holders make the most money. The diggers are entitled to receive a percentage, but by the time operating expenses and their debts for food and clothing are deducted, there is usually little left. The reduction in the number of farm laborers means less rice (the staple food) is raised, requiring the government to import it.

Most of the people are animists or nominal Muslims, but the percentage of practicing Muslims is higher than the national average. A mosque or two can be found in every diamond mining town plus numerous praying groups, each worshipping on a piece of ground shaped, by the use of logs or inverted bottles, like a mosque and facing east.

Christians have also left their homes in search of work in the diamond mines. Many of them are only nominal Christians, but others were active in their home churches and have continued being active in the mining towns. All along the upper Sewa, and in Konoland, small congregations have emerged with their own leadership, but the membership is unstable and attendance fluctuates greatly from week to week.

From one point of view, this new class in these emerging mining towns presents a great opportunity for the Church because they are away from family ties which might hinder conversion. But the experience of the author has shown that this new class is not responsive. The goal for them is money; for many, stealing is a way of life; and their transient nature makes pastoral follow-up difficult and sometimes impossible.

It is in such religious groupings, social structures, and economic and demographic factors that the Gospel is being proclaimed and churches are — and are not — being planted.

The whole following history of church expansion in Sierra Leone must be seen against these realities. Only so, can the outcomes be understood.

# PART II
# THE CHURCH

# CHAPTER 4

# HISTORICAL SUMMARY

## BEGINNINGS

The first Protestant Churches in Sierra Leone began with the arrival of the Settlers from Nova Scotia in 1792. Among the Settlers were Baptists, Methodists, and members of the Countess of Huntingdon's Connexion. As they had their own Negro preachers, each denomination continued in Sierra Leone without any European supervision.

The late 1700s and early 1800s saw the formation of the first Protestant missionary societies. The first attempts to begin missionary work in Africa were failures. Sierra Leone was chosen because the slave trade was illegal there and because the societies had the support of the Sierra Leone Company directors.

In December, 1795, the Baptists in England sent two missionaries. One returned because of illness and the other went to America after being expelled from the Colony for meddling in government affairs. In 1796, the Glasgow Missionary Society also sent two men. The same year, Dr. Coke, the father of Wesleyan missions, sent a team to civilize the Fulani through community development. But after the team arrived in the Colony the primitive conditions and the magnitude of the task so overwhelmed them that they all resigned.

In 1799, three societies, the London Missionary Society, the Edinburgh Missionary Society, and the Glasgow Missionary Society, tried a joint effort, each sending two missionaries. Because the men quarreled on the way, upon their arrival

* I am indebted to C. P. Groves, Harvey Newcomb, and K. S. Latourette for the information contained in chapters four and five regarding the history of the Church in Sierra Leone.

the governor stationed them far apart — on the Rio Pongas, sixty miles north of Freetown; in the Banana Islands, forty miles south of Freetown, and with the Bullom people, across the estuary from Freetown. Three died from sickness; one was murdered by itinerant Fula traders; one returned because of sickness, and the other was recalled as not fit for the work. None of these three societies ever resumed work in Sierra Leone.

The British Methodists, however, tried again. A Methodist congregation was already in Sierra Leone because of the Settlers from Nova Scotia. From time to time unofficial missionaries came to Sierra Leone and gave assistance. The year 1797 saw four hundred Methodists in Sierra Leone, of whom 223 were blacks and mulattoes. In 1804 the little flock was being served by three local preachers, two English and one Negro. The Negro worked among the Maroons. In 1808 the total number of church members was one hundred. Three years later Dr. Coke sent an ordained missionary to superintend the work. Eighty-nine years later, in 1900, the Wesleyan Methodist Missionary Society began successful work among the tribal people (the Mende).

The Church Missionary Society took twelve years and three tries to establish a permanent work in Africa. Their first attempt, in 1804, failed when the two Germans they sent from Berlin Mission Seminary became chaplains in the Colony instead of working among the Susu where they were meant to go.

The second attempt was in 1808 when the Society sent three new missionaries to the Rio Pongas. The mission lasted eight years and increased to three stations. However, since the missionaries believed it was impossible to convert the adults or do them good in any way "... they did not attempt to preach, but confined their efforts to the children, thus erroneously limiting the power of the gospel" (Newcomb 1854: 65). Thus there was no church, no proper public worship, and no itinerant preaching.

The third attempt began in 1816 when the three stations were closed and the missionaries, with most of their pupils (liberated Africans), moved to the Colony. The hostility of the slave traders was the main reason for the move. Along with the change of location was a change of policy. Hereafter missionaries should preach the Gospel. The Church Missionary Society then began work among the liberated Africans of the Colony but never succeeded in establishing permanent work among the tribal people.

The first missions to the Mende and Sherbro people were begun by the American Missionary Association. Some Mende had been sold into slavery and resold at Havana, Cuba, to some Spaniards. While the Spaniards were carrying them on the schooner Amistead, the Mende mutinied and captured the ship. In 1839 the schooner was seized by the American Navy. Two Spaniards were still alive and one of them claimed the forty Africans as his. Two years later the Mende, in a historic court decision, were declared free. In the meantime they had received some instruction that included Christianity, and when they were permitted to return to their homeland, they wanted some of their Christian teachers to accompany them. Consequently, the American Missionary Association sent two missionaries with them to Sierra Leone, where they arrived in January, 1842. By November the first station was opened at Kaw Mendi. Three years later a tribal war began and the mission station became a place of refuge. Between 1848 and 1854 nineteen missionaries, some with wives, were sent to the mission. The death toll was high. (See page 70 for the 1854 statistics of the mission.) The work was transferred to the Evangelical United Brethren Mission in 1882 because this group had missionary work adjacent to it. Tissana became a Methodist station in 1922.

In 1850 the Evangelical United Brethren Church* began work among the Sherbro. They now have churches among the Mende, Temne, Sherbro, Kono, and Kissi. In 1889 the American Wesleyan Methodist Church established work among the Limba, and now has churches among the Susu, Limba, Temne, and Loko. In 1897 the United Brethren in Christ Church commenced work among the Mende.

* Before 1889 the Evangelical United Brethren and the United Brethren in Christ were one, called United Brethren in Christ. In 1889 the Church split. The part which retained the work in Sierra Leone kept the name United Brethren in Christ. In 1946 it merged with the Evangelical Association and changed its name to Evangelical United Brethren. The part of the Church which lost the work in Sierra Leone took

## AMERICAN MISSIONARY ASSOCIATION

### Statistics for 1854

| Stations | Time of Commencing | Ordained Missionaries | Male Assistants | Female Assistants | Native Assistants | Churches | Members | Schools | Scholars |
|---|---|---|---|---|---|---|---|---|---|
| Kaw-Mendi - - - - - | 1842 | 2 | 2 | 4 | 1 | 1 | 34 | 1 | 80 |
| Good Hope - - - - - | 1853 | 2 | 1 | 2 | | | | | |
| Mo-Tappan - - - - - | 1853 | | 1 | 1 | 2 | 1 | 6 | 1 | |
| Total - - - - | | 4 | 4 | 7 | 3 | 2 | 40 | 2 | 80 |

(Source: Newcomb, _Cyclopedia of Missions_ 1854)

See the map on page 71 for the location of these Churches according to the comity agreement of 1927. The Missionary Church Association, which works with the Koranko, Yalunka,

the name United Brethren in Christ Old Constitution. In 1897 this part began work in Sierra Leone under the name United Brethren of America. In 1946 the United Brethren of America Mission changed its name back to United Brethren in Christ.

To prevent confusion, I shall use the name Evangelical United Brethren to refer to all its missionary work from its beginning in 1850. And I shall use the name United Brethren in Christ to refer to all United Brethren in Christ missionary work after its organization in 1926.

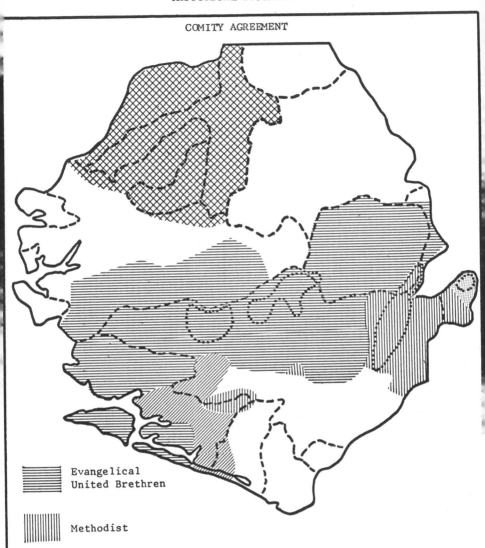

COMITY AGREEMENT

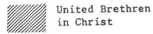 Evangelical
United Brethren

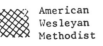 Methodist

United Brethren
in Christ

American
Wesleyan
Methodist

 Assemblies
Of God

- - - - - Tribal Boundaries

. . . . . Boundaries of truly occupied
territory, that is, territory
with a group of Christians in
almost every village

# PROTESTANT POPULATION AND COMMUNITY

## FIGURES

## 1962

| Creole Churches | Community |
|---|---|
| African Methodist Episcopal | 500* |
| Countess of Huntingdon | 2,000* |
| Methodist (Creole) | 13,500* |
| Sierra Leone Church (Anglican) | 15,500 |
| West African Methodist | 2,000* |
| | 33,500 |

### Tribal Churches

| | |
|---|---|
| American Wesleyan Methodist | 5,600 |
| Assemblies of God (Kru) | 700* |
| Assemblies of God (Kissi) | 700 |
| Church of God of Prophecy | 2,400 |
| Evangelical United Brethren | 21,000 |
| Methodist (Mende) | 7,000 |
| Missionary Church Association | 400 |
| Seventh-day Adventist | 4,100 |
| United Brethren in Christ | 3,000 |
| United Pentecostal | 800* |
| | 45,700 |

Grand Total    79,200

Christian Community figures are based on
official 1962 statistics of the individual
Churches, i.e., the number of Communicants
or Baptized Adults for the various Churche
have been doubled.

Because there were no official statistics
available for those Churches marked with a
asterisk (*), figures listed in
the World Christian Handbook,
1962 (London: World Dominion
Press) were used.

Population figures are from the
1963 Census.

Total Population
2,180,356    3.6%

Tribal Population
2,130,356    2.1%

Creole Population
50,000 (est.)    67%

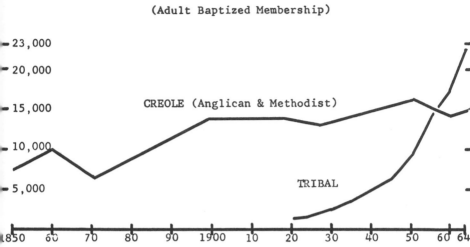

COMPARISON OF CREOLE AND TRIBAL CHURCHES

(Adult Baptized Membership)

The growth line of the tribal Churches shows where the growth of the Church now is occurring. The line is pointing up--showing that the tribes are ready for harvest into the Kingdom of God.

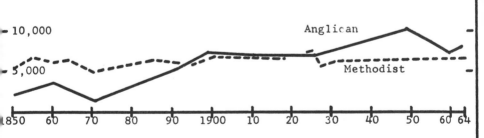

COMPARISON OF CREOLE CHURCHES

(Anglican and Methodist)

This graph shows the discipling of the Creoles. The Sierra Leone Church (Anglican) experienced a slow rise in membership, with a long plateau of no growth for thirty years, from 1900 to 1930. The Methodist Creole Church has had no growth after its first fifty-five years of rapid growth (from 1811 to 1855, not shown on the graph). The fact that 67% of the Creoles are Christian means the Creoles are well discipled, and have been since 1900.

# COMPARISON OF TRIBAL CHURCHES

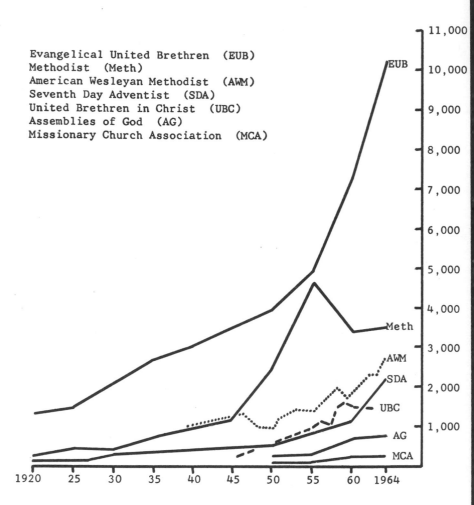

Evangelical United Brethren  (EUB)
Methodist  (Meth)
American Wesleyan Methodist  (AWM)
Seventh Day Adventist  (SDA)
United Brethren in Christ  (UBC)
Assemblies of God  (AG)
Missionary Church Association  (MCA)

These lines show that church growth among the tribes varies greatly from Church to Church. Yet the people among whom the Churches work are fairly uniform in their cultural and religious backgrounds. The MCAs have made hardly any impact, while the EUBs have made comparatively great gains. From 1945 to 1955 the EUBs had slow growth--a gain of 1453, or 40.9%, while the Methodists soared--a gain of 3509, or 248.9%. After 1955 the EUBs soared--gaining 5160, or 103.6%, while the Methodists lost--losing 1192, or 25.3%. In the following chapters we will examine each Church more closely to discover why.

and Temne tribes, is not shown because its churches are few and scattered. The Seventh-day Adventists do not observe comity and their churches are scattered in the Evangelical United Brethren area, and to the north among the Temne.

## FIELD GROWTH

Since 1811 there has been Christian missionary work in the Western Area, and in the Provinces since 1842. What has been the result of this missionary endeavor of more than a century? The bar graphs on page 72 show the Protestant Christian Community in relation to the total, the tribal, and the Creole populations. The Creole population in the Western Area is 25 per cent of the total. Although 67 per cent of the Creoles are within the Christian community, only 17 per cent of the Western Area is Christian. *The bar graphs show only a bare beginning in discipling the tribal people of Sierra Leone.*

I emphasize this because when I arrived in Sierra Leone as a new missionary, I received the impression from many church leaders that one-third of the population of Sierra Leone was Christian. All the Evangelical United Brethren ministers serve town churches and spend most of their time with Christians. This is true of most Churches. Many leaders are unaware of the cultural and religious conditions in which thousands upon thousands of tribesmen live. Policy is made as though all churches were town churches. Village churches — which are the *only means* through which the millions of non-Christian tribesmen can be won — and their problems, are almost completely ignored.

The next question we must ask is, How have these Churches grown? That is, over the years, what has been their numerical growth? The line graphs on pages 73 and 74 show the comparative growth of (1) the Creole and the tribal Churches, (2) the Anglican Creole (Sierra Leone Church) and the Methodist Creole, and (3) the tribal Churches of the various denominations. The figures are from communicant membership statistics. (The figures for the Methodist Church comprise all baptized adults.)

Later we will see in more detail how the various sections of the Methodist Mende Church and the Evangelical United

Brethren Church have grown. Line graphs based on field totals show an overall picture of growth but fail to show which individual churches or areas are growing well and which are not. This is because the statistics of all the churches, from the dying ones to the rapidly growing, are combined.

Only 2.1 per cent of the tribesmen of Sierra Leone are Christian (Protestant), and most of them are concentrated into a few small areas. Yet, the 2.1 per cent is a firm foundation from which the Churches and their assisting missions can — if they set their minds to achieving a workable strategy — claim the tribes for Christ.

# CHAPTER 5

# THE SIERRA LEONE CHURCH
# (ANGLICAN-CREOLE)

## BEGINNINGS

The story of the Anglican Church in Sierra Leone begins with the liberated Africans. Although most of the Settlers were Christians, none was Anglican. In 1816 the Church Missionary Society transferred its missionaries to Sierra Leone and sent out four new missionary couples. The two outstanding ones were Johnson and During. Although they had been instructed by the Society not to preach, they followed the advice of the secretary of the Society and preached anyway. Johnson was stationed at Regent's Town, where he faced very discouraging conditions:

> Natives of 22 different nations were collected together, mostly taken from the holds of slave-ships. They were in a state of continual hostility, with no means of communicating with each other, but a little broken English. When clothing was given them, they would sell it, or throw it away. None of them lived in the married state, but they herded together like brutes. From ten to twenty of them were crowded together in a single hut. Many of them were ghastly as skeletons, and six or eight of them sometimes died in a day. Only six children were born in a year. Superstition tyrannized over their minds, and there was little desire for instruction. Hardly any land was cultivated by them. Some would live by themselves in the woods, and others subsisted by thieving and plunder. Many of them would prefer any kind of refuse meat to the rations they received from Government.
>
> So many negroes continued to arrive from slave vessels, that Mr. Johnson had to issue rations twice a week for a thousand persons. He was greatly tried with their indifference,

when he attempted to preach Christ to them, and was often on the point of giving up in discouragement (Newcomb 1854: 65-66).

## PEOPLE MOVEMENTS

But gradually there was improvement. The year after Johnson arrived saw a people movement at his station, at During's in Gloucester, and at several others.

> Young persons were seen retiring to the woods for prayer, and little groups assembled by moonlight to chant the praises of the Redeemer. Both old and young appeared anxious to be instructed in the way of salvation. Polygamy, greegrees (charms), and the worship of the devil were universally abandoned (Newcomb 1854: 66).

In that year, 1817, the villages of the Colony were divided into thirteen parishes, each to have a minister and a schoolmaster. The Society was to provide the personnel while the government would largely find the funds.

The growth in the membership of the Church was not due to easy admission. C. P. Groves tells of Johnson's disagreement with the governor on the matter of baptism:

> Johnson had standards which he would not relax. Inquirers, accepted as catechumens, were received in the presence of the communicant members, who were desired to watch over them and report on the sincerity of their intentions as observable in their conduct. Thus the period of preparation became a responsibility of the whole church. Catechumens remained some four to five months under instruction, according to the progress made. Johnson himself and African helpers instructed them twice a week. The rite of baptism was preceded by a public questioning before the whole congregation. He declined to baptize without previous instruction, and only received for this purpose those who had an evident spiritual concern. This careful policy brought him into collision with McCarthy (the Governor). He reports in his journal for May 13, 1818: "His Excellency the Governor came here to-day. He led the conversation while we were in the garden to baptism. He wished I would baptize more people. I told him that I could not, unless God first baptized their hearts. He said that the reason so many were baptized on the day of Pentecost was that the Apostles despised none.

I replied that they were pricked in the heart, and that I was willing to baptize all that were thus pricked in the heart. He thought baptism an act of civilization, and that it was our duty to make them all Christians. He spoke in great warmth about these things, and I endeavoured to show him through Scripture passages, the contrary. He gave it up at last; calling me and the Society a set of fanatics." With all their confidence in Johnson, the Secretaries began to wonder whether he was not pitching his standard too high, and wrote him: "The Committee have been disposed to think, from the Governor's representations, that you may have been rather too slow to baptize, making all due allowance for his not having our views and feelings" (1954: 277-78).

Besides being a preacher and schoolmaster, Johnson helped the government by overseeing the distribution of clothing and food to the desperately needy liberated Africans of Regent's Town until they had time to stand on their own feet. He was also involved in job training. "We have now," Johnson reported in 1817, "masons, bricklayers, carpenters, shinglemakers, sawyers, smiths, tailors and brickmakers" (Groves 1954: 279).

One means of evangelism was the influence of converted liberated Africans upon their friends and relatives who had been captured and then later liberated in Freetown. In 1821 Johnson brought some newly liberated Africans to Regent's Town. He wrote of the resulting scene,

I cannot describe the scenes which occurred when we arrived at Regent's Town. I have seen many negroes landed, but never beheld such an affecting sight. . . . Many of our people recognized their friends and relatives, and there was a general cry, "Oh, massa, my sister!" "My brother!" "My sister!" "My countryman!" "My countrywoman!" . . . The poor creatures being faint — just taken out of the hold of a slave-vessel and unconscious of what had befallen them — did not know whether they should laugh or cry when they beheld the countenances of those whom they had supposed long dead, but now saw clothed and clean, and perhaps with healthy children in their arms (Groves 1954: 280).

## GOVERNMENT INTERFERENCE

In England the Church of England is subject to the State. Thus the program of the Church and education by the Church

Missionary Society in the Colony were partly controlled by the government. The arrangement (made in 1823 or 1824) was that the Society was to recruit and pay salaries to all the English clergymen of the Colony, subject of course to the approval of the Secretary of State; the government was to provide materials for educating the liberated Africans and housing for the teachers, and furnish dwellings for the clergy and chapels.

The government fulfilled the former but not the latter. Further, the governor had his own ideas as to how long boys were to remain in school. He directed that when they reached ten or twelve years of age they should leave school and go to work. Also, he released the missionaries from managing the schools. As a result the missionaries began establishing their own schools as the Methodists were doing. In 1846 the Society formally ended its agreement with the government.

## CREOLE CLERGY

The Society experienced a great drain on missionary personnel through frequent deaths. At the close of the first twenty years (1824) only twenty-seven of seventy missionaries sent out were alive, and some of these were totally unfit for missionary work. This taught the Society the necessity and value of an indigenous leadership. In 1827 Fourah Bay College was started. The first ordination of Creole clergy took place in 1852, the year Sierra Leone received its first bishop. Thereafter there was a steady supply of Creole clergy. Gradually the churches of the Colony were staffed by Creoles, and by 1860, when the Sierra Leone Native Pastorate was formed, there were enough clergy to staff the entire colony area. The thirteen stations were staffed by twelve Creole clergymen, who served 3,797 communicants and preached to an average congregation of 7,173.

## CREOLE MISSIONARY ENDEAVOR

Converted Africans are better able to convey the Gospel meaningfully to fellow Africans than are Europeans. The missionaries soon realized this when they saw unconverted liberated Africans readily receive the words of those converted.

The missionaries praised God for this. The liberated Africans, in 1853, were from 200 different tribes speaking 150 separate languages plus many dialects. Not only would these men be able to evangelize Sierra Leone but all of Africa.

The missionaries therefore began educating African helpers and learning some of the languages. In 1829 they began putting the languages into writing. By 1853 the Scriptures and some elementary works had been translated into Temne, Hausa, Yoruba, and Susu.

Bullom, opposite the estuary from Freetown, was the first area reached. In 1840 a station was opened at Port Loko, in Temneland, but strong Islam influence prevented the acceptance of the Gospel. In 1853 a liberated African was placed in charge, and in 1895 a campaign was launched to evangelize the Temne. Within a year, European and Creole missionaries opened more than a dozen stations in the main towns of the western third of Temneland (see map on page 26). But two years later, in 1898, all the work was closed because of the Hut Tax War, and only Port Loko was reopened after the war.

In 1861 the Church Missionary Society began work among the Temne in Quiah, an area on the eastern boundary of the Colony. In 1876 this work and also that at Bullom were turned over to the newly formed Sierra Leone Church Mission.

In 1894 the Creole congregation at Bonthe, on Sherbro Island, began evangelizing the people with whom its members were trading. It sent missionary couples out to three trading centers. By 1896 the Sierra Leone Church Mission, noting the progress of this venture of the Bonthe congregation, began to share their concern, and within a year opened two stations. The following year the Hut Tax War closed the stations. Efforts were made to resume the work after the war, but without success.

In the extreme north of the country the Church Missionary Society opened the Falaba Mission among the Yalunka in 1898. This mission made contact with the Limba and Koranko tribes as well as the Yalunka. There were no results until 1906, when two converts were baptized. In that same year the missionaries (European and Creole) translated the Gospel according to Matthew and a reading book containing the Lord's

Prayer, the Apostles' Creed, the Ten Commandments, and some simple New Testament stories. The following year the Church Missionary Society turned this mission, its last post in the hinterland, over to the Sierra Leone Church Mission and confined its missionaries to working in the educational institutions in Freetown. Five years later the Sierra Leone Church also withdrew, allegedly because of transportation difficulties.

The year 1912 saw the last of the Sierra Leone Church efforts to evangelize the tribes. The churches that remained (Quiah, Bullom, and Port Loko) had become Creole. The Hut Tax War and the lack of response from the natives confirmed the Creole belief that the natives were savages who would not become Christian.

By 1916 the Sierra Leone Railway was under construction from Freetown to Bo, then on to Pendembu through Mendeland. Creole traders followed the railway, settled in the trading centers, and formed themselves into Anglican congregations. But they did no evangelism of the tribal people. Four of the towns in which they had churches (Daru, Gerihun, Panguma, and Kailahun), some of them at a distance from the railway, were handed over to other missions in 1927 as a result of comity arrangements made under the United Christian Council of Sierra Leone.

The Church Missionary Society missionaries had high hopes that through the help of the converted liberated Africans they would be able to evangelize Sierra Leone. They failed. One must therefore ask, Was it good strategy for the Church Missionary Society to turn its entire work over to the Sierra Leone Church? The answer will be discussed after we examine the other Creole Churches.

## INFLUENCE OF ANGLICAN CREOLES

The Anglicans did not succeed in establishing tribal churches. Nevertheless, they had a marked effect upon the life of other Churches. Their greatest effect was on the Methodist Church, among the Creoles. Against the wishes of the Methodist missionaries, the Methodist Creole churches were adopting more and more elaborate, ritualistic worship forms. This use of Anglican worship forms did not spread beyond the Creoles, but their marriage patterns and theology influenced several other Churches.

*Christian Marriages*

On June 1, 1848, George Thompson (of the American Missionary Association, Mende Mission) witnessed a wedding party in Freetown. He wrote concerning it:

> The bride and her attendants were adorned with excessive richness and extravagance, while others around were half naked. The party sat down to a table in the open air, loaded with a great variety of delicate and costly viands.
>
> In Sierra Leone custom has the force of law, and any person who gets married, must go to all this expense and parade — the most extravagant and costly dress, the richest articles of food and luxury, intoxicating drinks, and a company of attendants. So that it often takes the savings of *years* to be able to get married — and sometimes runs the party in *debt,* into *prison* and *ruin:* and few can be found who *go against* this ridiculous, slavish custom (1859: 31).

Coupled with the ceremony is the practice of registering the marriage with the government. Many churchmen in high positions to this day, both Creole and tribal, feel that a marriage is not valid in the eyes of the Church or God unless it is sanctified by a ceremony patterned after European marriage customs and registered with the government according to civil law. This feeling reveals itself in the official attitude of several Churches.

One United Brethren in Christ preacher I interviewed said none of his church members was married and were all living in fornication except himself and his wife, because none had been married in the church. They were, however, legally married according to tradition and Sierra Leone law. A married, unordained, paid preacher of the Evangelical United Brethren Church, when asked if he were married, said, "No," answering according to the official church definition of marriage. He knew that before God, the community, and the local church he was married, but that before the top officials of his Church he was not.

This attitude toward marriage prevents the general membership of the Church from having a Christian understanding of the marriage relationship. A church wedding is understood as something done to please high church officials or, in cases of townspeople, to achieve status. Church officials stress government-registered weddings to make divorce difficult. The emphasis is on prevention of divorce rather than on the Christian home. As a result, most tribal Christians (who belong to Churches which provide only for government-registered weddings) do not get "married."

By contrast, surely Christians must hold that the true purpose of church weddings is for couples to vow to each other and before the congregation to be faithful to each other and establish Christian homes in which Christ is honored and in which children will be brought up to know and love Him.

Such church weddings do not need to be registered with the government unless the government so requires. The Methodists have a ceremony whereby monogamous Christians who are married according to tradition may make vows to be faithful and to establish Christian homes. By this ceremony the Methodists are in a position to teach Christian family responsibilities. On the other hand, the Evangelical United Brethren Church, for example, has rejected such ceremonies in favor of government-registered church weddings and has thereby prevented most of its maried members from vowing to establish Christian homes. This has greatly handicapped its ministers in their task of Christian education.

A wedding would be just as sacred, and would surely be more meaningful to the couples involved and to the Christians of the local church, if it were performed with simple vows, within the local church or local congregation. Such church weddings would confirm and sanctify marriages validated in the traditional way.

I stress "validated" to indicate I am referring to only one kind of traditional marriage. For example, among the Mende there are at least three kinds. Two are temporary but socially accepted unions.* The other is an agreement between two persons and their families validated by the giving of gifts

* The two temporary unions are (1) a man and woman living together without family knowledge or approval, and (2) an arrangement whereby an unmarried man working for a polygamous household receives one of the women of the house as his companion.

(commonly called bride price or bride wealth). Marriages of the third kind among Christian couples should be dedicated to God in simple church ceremonies.

Another custom which has influenced the educated tribal churchmen is the christening of babies, which is usually followed by a party with drinking and dancing.

S. A. J. Pratt, a prominent Creole layman of the Sierra Leone Church, said of the Churches operating in the hinterland, "These did magnificent evangelistic work in the past, until they followed the pattern of the Colony Churches and concentrated their ministry mainly on converted Christians" (1956: 161).

# CHAPTER 6

# THE METHODIST CREOLE CHURCH (BRITISH)

This chapter highlights the history of the Methodist Church among the Creoles, and the Wesleyan Missionary Society's efforts to achieve tribal work.

The Methodist Church has two categories of members: (1) Members on Trial, who have been baptized and are receiving further instruction in preparation for becoming (2) Full Members, who may receive communion and hold office in the church. Another category within the church is the catechumenate. Catechumens are converts who have enrolled to receive instruction which prepares them for baptism.

The Creoles underwent rapid ingathering until 1857. The Methodists experienced people movements among the liberated Africans similar to those of the Anglicans. In 1852 the missionaries reported to the London Committee that at Murraytown "idolaters were giving up their idols." Voluntarily the people had given up their idols to the constable, until his veranda was "full of idols and other superstitious stuff." The movement spread to Freetown. Newcomb relates:

> At Free Town such a number of idols were given up as no one suspected the place to have contained. The people took the matter into their own hands, and seemed to be simultaneously moved by an invisible impulse, becoming such enthusiastic Iconoclasts, that Mr. Fletcher [the missionary] tells us all other work was suspended. In crowds, but not tumultuously, they paraded through the streets, carrying the

---

* All information for this section is from the "Synod Minutes of the Methodist Church — Sierra Leone" unless otherwise noted. The Synod Minutes are in manuscript form in the archives of the Methodist Missionary Society, London.

heathen deities in procession, to deliver them up to the magistrates and missionaries. Mr. Fletcher turned his apartments into a museum for the exhibition of those unsightly abominations, and thousands of people came to look at them. The fame of this movement has spread far along the coast, producing deep impressions among the various tribes . . . (1854: 178).

The drop in membership in 1857 corresponds with the implementation of the catechumenal system. Catechumens usually form the growing edge of a Church, i.e., in churches which grow through conversions from the world (people with a non-Christian background), the rise and fall of the full membership is usually related directly to the number of catechumens.

Among the Creoles this principle appears generally to be true. As the catechumenal segment widens, the membership increases, and vice versa. However, in Sierra Leone the great ingathering occurred before the catechumenal system was introduced. Thereafter the number of adult baptisms, or conversions from the world, steadily decreased, and the number of infants baptized increased until, in the year 1900, only thirty-eight adults and 314 infants were baptized.

Someone should investigate why the catechumenal system was introduced by the Methodists, what effect it had upon this Creole Church, and who were being catechized — individuals from the world or children of the members. The minutes of the Church for 1851, when the pattern of rapid church growth was still active, indicate that some churches were having catechism classes. After that the growth began to taper off, and stopped in 1857. In this year the mission headquarters in London sent statistical return forms which included a column for catechumens. The investigation should discover what the baptismal requirements were before the introduction of the catechumenal system, and whether they were changed and became more demanding afterwards. The Church Missionary Society had catechumen classes and its Church grew more gradually than did the Methodist's. There may be a correlation.

Two other things occurred about that time which may have affected the growth. In 1855 there was a reduction in funds from England; and in 1857 the missionaries said the Colony was well churched, with no more place for stations. The investigation should inquire into what effect these two factors had on the drop in membership.

The drop in 1867 was due to purging backsliders and nonresidents from the rolls. After the roll correction a general increase followed until the peak of full members in 1920.

A study of the Methodist work among the Limba and Temne reveals that the number of catechumens bears no relationship to the membership of the churches. Compared with the beginning of the Creole work, these missions started well. The first nine years of the Limba and Temne missions saw greater growth than did the first nine years of the Creole mission beginning in 1811.

But after nine years the Limba War started, and the churches suffered loss for four years. After the war the membership gained for two years, then declined during the Hut Tax War. The membership never rose after that, but the number of catechumens did. The rise in the number of catechumens after 1900 may indicate the beginning of a people movement to Christ among the Limba, but only a handful were baptized. Most of the baptisms were of children. From 1900 to 1915, during the rise in number of catechumens, twenty-seven adults and sixty-eight infants were baptized in the Limba mission; twenty-four adults and 122 infants were baptized in the Temne mission. Two wars did not stop the people's desire to turn to Christ.

*The records indicate responsiveness among the Limba and Temne, but little or no follow-up.* The history of missions around the world relates numerous cases in which missionaries did not recognize a responsive people ready for harvest, with the result that the harvest was lost — *and souls were lost forever.* National church leaders and missionaries must be alert to find responsive peoples, and then must concentrate their forces to reap the harvest until the last soul is brought into the Kingdom of God.

## HISTORICAL HIGHLIGHTS

We now turn to the highlights of the Methodist Church as it built up the Creole Church and sought to begin a tribal Church.

The first official Methodist missionaries arrived in Sierra Leone November 12, 1811, and found some Methodist Nova Scotians holding services. Soon after their arrival the Maroon Chapel (an independent church which had grown among the Maroons from the West Indies) joined the Methodist connection. Except for the Maroons and a few Nova Scotians, the missionaries worked among the liberated Africans.

In 1843, sixteen years after the Anglicans had started Fourah Bay College, the Wesleyan Educational and Theological Institution was established to train Methodist members for the ministry and for general usefulness in the Church. The 1850 "Report of the Native Training Institution" (as it was then called) declared its hope that the Institution would prove "a powerful auxiliary in the spread of evangelical truth, not only throughout this colony, but also throughout the regions beyond. . . ."

To accomplish this hope the course of studies included: theology, Latin, Greek, English grammar, composition, ancient and modern history, arithmetic, geography with the use of the globe, and natural philosophy. Although this was excellent education for the Creoles who desired to become Europeanized, it did not equip them to evangelize "the regions beyond" where the animists were.

The structure of the Church is revealed in the "General Returns" for 1843.

As the table indicates, the Methodists divided their congregations into small classes, or cells, for more effective instruction, fellowship, and pastoral care and used laymen (unpaid agents) to conduct class meetings. The chart also indicates use of the school approach (note the number of day school teachers). At this time the Mission supported the missionaries, the schools, and the teachers; the local churches supported the other paid agents.

The plan of the Church to evangelize the Colony was for each pastor to visit all the towns and villages around his station until churches were planted in them. At the annual District Meeting, one of the questions on the questionnaire from London was: "What towns or villages in the neighborhood of each station are not visited and give the reasons why they are not, and whether the said reasons are satisfactory to the

| | Stations or Circuits | Freetown | Hastings and Wellington | York | Total |
|---|---|---|---|---|---|
| | No. of Chapels | 15 | 7 | 6 | 28 |
| | No. of Missionaries and Assistants | 3 | 1 | 1 | 5 |
| Subordinate Paid Agents | Catechists Readers Interpreters | 144 | 30 | 10 | 184 |
| | Day School Teachers | 17 | 9 | 4 | 30 |
| Unpaid Agents | Sabbath School Teachers | 20 | 2 | 10 | 32 |
| | Preachers or Exhorters | 41 | 4 | 4 | 49 |
| | Class Leaders | 70 | 19 | 11 | 100 |
| Members | Full | 1898 | 510 | 289 | 2697 |
| | On Trial | 379 | 120 | 75 | 574 |
| | Total Membership | 2277 | 630 | 364 | 3271 |

brethren of the District?" The answer to this question usually was, "We extend our labours as far as it is practicable," indicating that some towns and villages were not being visited (Synod Minutes 1850).

Pastoral work, besides regular meetings under the class leader, included a quarterly visit by the man in charge of the circuit to each class "to acquaint himself with the state of each member and to give suitable advice to each." No other language than English was used since the work was only in the Colony (Synod Minutes 1845).

The January 11, 1855, report reveals the heavy dependence of the Methodist Church upon funds from England. The Conference Committee in England* told the Sierra Leone District of difficult finances at home and requested the district to (1) keep expenditures within the grant of £1350 per annum, (2) increase school fees, (3) pay for their own chapel construction and repairs, and (4) pay for salaries. The District Committee replied that the parents of school children were too poor to increase the weekly payment. They went on to say that the Conference Committee erred in thinking that the people could build and repair their own chapels and that unless the Committee granted a sum of £50 annually for repairs, the chapels

* To avoid confusion I offer the following explanation of Methodist organization and terminology.

*Conference* refers to the annual business meeting of the Methodist Church in England. The *Conference Committee* is the executive committee of conference members which meets between annual sessions of the Conference and is amenable to it. The Methodist Church in Sierra Leone was a *District* of the English Conference, its ministers and lay representatives meeting annually as a *Synod*. The *District Committee* is the executive committee of Synod members which meets between annual sessions of the Synod. This is the church structure. (In 1967 Sierra Leone became a separate conference with two districts, Western and Provincial.)

A mission structure also operates. The *Methodist Missionary Society* (formerly called Wesleyan Missionary Society, and then Wesleyan Methodist Missionary Society) is the missionary organization of the Methodist Church in Britain and is amenable to the Conference. Its executive committee is the *London Committee* through which it administers its many overseas missions, including Sierra Leone.

Thus the Sierra Leone District, being both church and mission, was amenable to both the English Conference Committee and the London Committee, with the English Conference having the final authority.

would fall, to the disgrace of Methodism. As a result, several day schools were given up, some teachers were dismissed, and the number of students at the Native Training Institution was reduced.

The liberated Africans had nothing when they arrived. Many of them — men, women, and children — did not even have a stitch of clothing. They were entirely dependent upon the government and the missionaries to get a start in the Colony. This pattern of dependence carried over into church affairs. Yet, by the end of 1854, there were 6,828 members divided among thirty-four chapels in four circuits.

The cry of the missionaries to their home board, pleading for financial help because of the poverty and inability of the people to help themselves, is the same cry heard today among the educated churchmen to their church leaders. They have been so accustomed to being told they cannot help themselves that they have come to believe it. Once the pattern of dependence is set it is difficult to eradicate it.

One of the problems the missionaries faced in 1855, besides the poverty of the church members, was their ideal that a church building should look like those in England. Also, the missionaries were concerned about Methodism being disgraced. This attitude of pride in, and fear of disgrace for, one's denomination has persisted and is alive today in the various denominations in Sierra Léone. Church leaders often have more concern for the prestige of their respective denominations than they have for discipling peoples and making them responsible members of Christ's Church.

In 1857 the missionaries on the field declared that the Colony was well churched and that the London Committee should "afford the means of extending the Mission into the interior of this vast Continent as we think the time has fully come when such a course should be pursued."* However, *only the English-speaking towns* in the Colony were being reached.

* Question No. 36 in the Jan. 13, 1857, minutes reads: "Are there any new stations to be recommended to the attention of the committee?" The answer reads: "We have no new stations within the boundaries of the colony to recommend. There are numerous openings among the surrounding tribes where Missionaries could be placed and

In 1866 the London Committee requested that the Sierra Leone District be turned over to the native Church and be self-supporting, since finances were so difficult in England. The Committee was referring to the Sierra Leone Native Pastorate Church which the Church Missionary Society had formed three years earlier. The District Committee replied,

> ... for the information and kind consideration of the (London) Committee, — 1. That *all* the Churches of the Church Missionary Society are not so transferred. 2. Nor are those transferred *wholly* self-supporting; there being what is called the 'Bishop's Fund,' besides an Annual Grant from the Missionary Committee in England, to meet the Deficiency. 3. Nor are all the native Agents included in what is termed the Native Pastorate, as some of the native Ministers, and all the Catechists remain connected with the Church Missionary Society.

In 1867 the Sierra Leone District was placed under native administration, but the chairman and general superintendent was still a missionary appointed by the Conference in England.

## TRIBAL MISSIONS BEGUN

The following year, 1877, marked the beginning of efforts to achieve tribal work. Within four years missions were begun in three different language areas. The process can best be seen in the following time chart of each mission. (See the map on page 95 for the spread of this missionary endeavor.)

Sherbro Mission:

1877   A catechist is sent to Bonthe to gather the members of the Methodist Church who reside there, and begin a center of operations from which laborers might be sent into the neighboring Sherbro and Temne countries.

1878   A catechist is sent to Mokelleh, fifty miles from Bonthe.

where people would gladly receive them, but for the want of men to work the Stations we already have, we are precluded from entering the doors open to us, but we trust the [London] Committee will take the matter into their serious consideration and afford the means of extending the Mission into the interior. . . ."

1881    A Creole church is formed in Bonthe, but Mokelleh has no results.

1890    The work is progressing. The Creole catechist preaches and itinerates in Mende without an interpreter.

1899    The stations included in the Mission are: Bonthe, Moseley, York Island, Bandajuma, Morfuay, Yieleh, Bompeh, Imperreh.

1900    Bandajuma is separated from the Sherbro Mission and becomes an independent mission.

1910    The stations Yieleh, Bompeh, and Imperreh are closed. Those at Sombya and Gerahun are open.

1911    Sumbuya is separated from the Sherbro Mission and becomes the Sherbro Sumbuya Mission, and the Sherbro Mission is renamed the Sherbro-Bonthe Mission.

1918    Bonthe is no longer a mission, but a Creole circuit.

1933    The London Committee decides to send no more money for the Sherbro Mission.

Limba Mission:

1878    An English missionary attempts to open Limba country, but fails due to ill health.

1880    Another missionary is sent. He trains the chief's fifteen-year-old son (in Freetown), who learns English so well he becomes the missionary's interpreter. The town builds the missionary a house for £15, and a chapel free. A Creole catechist is sent to assist.

1884    The chief of Kambia fears that if a missionary comes and lives in his town the British government will annex his country. The Limba Mission includes Fouracarriah, the center, and four other stations.

1890    The Limba War is on in which twenty-eight towns and villages are destroyed, fifteen hundred people are slain or drowned, and seven hundred are sold into slavery. The missionary is assisting the Government Commissioner to establish peace.

1893    The Limba War is over.

1899    The four stations around Fouracarriah are not re-opened after the war. Kateri, Kambia, and Bullom (opposite Freetown) are added to the mission.

1906    The Limba Mission is divided. Kambia becomes the center of the new Scarcies Mission — among the Temne.

Methodist Church
Stations Occupied by 1922

1911   There is a circuit in Falaba among the Yalunka.*

1922   The Sierra Leone Synod (Creoles) are made responsible for the missions.

1937   Fouracarriah and Kambia are turned over to the American Wesleyan Methodist Church.

## Mabang (or Ribbi) Mission — Temne.

1880   A Creole catechist is sent to Mabang. He gathers a few Creoles into a class and itinerates. Two heathen begin "to pray" and the King (paramount chief) declares that he is a Christian.

1881   Practically all adherents are natives. They build a native-style chapel by themselves. Of the eight members, six are native and two Creole.

1890   A missionary is itinerating regularly, preaching in Temne and Mende.

1922   Six stations are listed, including Mabang.

1933   The London Committee decides to send no money for the Ribbi Mission.

## The Colony

1884   About nine thousand Temne-speaking pagans (with some Muslims) live within ten miles of a missionary stationed at Waterloo. The Creole agent there makes no effort to learn Temne or to relate to them, but ministers only to the handful of Creoles and English-speaking people. Arrangements are being made to supply the station with a more energetic and Temne-speaking catechist, and for a missionary to be stationed in Waterloo to direct the work.

In Freetown itself there are 3,396 Muslims and 2,018 pagans, besides soldiers. A missionary should be sent to do this work.

The colony churches say they need the annual grant to rebuild their churches or put them in repair and that if the grant is lessened the missionary work in the villages will suffer.

1893   Members from the Limba Mission, scattered by the

* The Synod Minutes make no mention of Falaba, but in the *Wesleyan Methodist Missionary Society* (1922: Vol. IV 103) six tribal circuits are noted for 1911: Bonthe, Fouracarriah, Gambia (Kambia), Mabang, Falaba, and Bandajuma.

war to the Colony, are being ministered to by the circuits there.

1894    Large numbers of aborigines are flooding into the Colony and particularly Freetown. Ten tribes are listed. Most of them are heathens, a few Muslims, and little has been done to reach them. A brother conversant in one or two languages should be entirely devoted to this work.

1920    City Mission is opened in Freetown.

1922    "There is an unwholesome congestion of the ministerial activity of our Church in the comparatively small area of the Peninsula."* Some should be sent into the interior.

1933    Wesleyan Methodist Church merges with the United Methodist Church.
The circuits Moyamba, Tikonko, and Banana Islands, and the church in Bo are added to the Methodist Church.

The Colony was strife-ridden in its early history. The natives (Temne) did not trust the newcomers. In 1922 the Wesleyan Methodist Missionary Society summed up the history and future of their work in Sierra Leone in these words:

These two classes of population were growing up foreigners to one another; alienations and jealousies were rife between them. In the colony itself there were racial divisions, whose differences generated feuds and caste prejudices, often of a bitter nature. The Nova Scotians and Maroons, the original nucleus of the settlement, looked down upon the later arrivals, who had come by shiploads [and] ... who imported with them numberless vices and superstitions. For many years the British cruisers brought in week by week new prizes over the harbour-bar, and released fresh cargoes of heathenism and barbarism. The work of the Church was constantly to do afresh. ... This perpetual renewal of the Missionary's and the schoolmaster's work at Sierra Leone was its wearing and disheartening feature. And it soon appeared that the Society could scarcely expect to do much beyond winning for Christ a certain number of emancipated Negroes; *little was to be accomplished through their aid in the near future in the way of affecting the Native heathen*

* Annual letter of the [London] Committee of the Sierra Leone District Synod (1922).

*folk, who must be appealed to on their own ground and through the medium of their mother-tongue.* The freed slaves remained utter strangers to the inhabitants of the shore where they landed, *their black hue did little or nothing to commend the new faith to their neighbours. Whatever success our Missionaries had with the Salleonians themselves, it became evident that their conversion would not directly help us far toward the winning of Negro Africa.* The liberated Africans lodged at Sierra Leone formed an *enclave* [italics not mine] by themselves through European hands, but whose gratitude went little farther, and who *had small idea of constituting themselves a missionary clan and being vehicles of Christ to their fellow countrymen. In this respect the Sierra Leone enterprise proved somewhat of a disappointment* (Wesleyan Methodist 1922:4:81; italics mine).

## Creoles No Longer Used

In that year, 1922, the London Committee realized that if they were to succeed in winning the tribal people they must not depend upon the Creoles, but must send missionaries to strike out on their own. All the circuits, except Bandajuma, were dominantly Creole. The London Committee therefore decided to concentrate in the Bandajuma area, or Mende Mission as it was then called. In the Annual Letter of the London Committee to the Sierra Leone Synod the Committee said:

> Our Grant for missionary work can only be employed for the Mende Mission. We have decided to withdraw from the Limba and Scarcies area. It is impossible for us with our present commitments effectively to develop and maintain work in two separate language areas and we must try to do one thing instead of doing two things very badly.
>
> We do not wish that the Christian congregations at Kambia and Fouracaria should be left desolate, and you as a Synod may be willing to undertake the care of these congregations. . . . It may be possible for the Committee, if you desire, to assume the financial responsibility for the Ribbi Mission thus constituting a compact area for its operations.

The Synod then assumed responsibility for the Limba and Scarcies missions. At that time the District Committee declared its intention to make those missions strong because "the time and opportunity are ripe for a great advance." We see from the graph that the area *was* ripe, but that the harvest was never brought in.

## EFFORTS TOWARD SELF-GOVERNMENT

Among the Mende we have seen the efforts to achieve a truly tribal mission succeeding. We now turn to the efforts of the Sierra Leone District Synod to achieve full self-government.

In 1876 the Church had been placed under native (Creole) administration, but the Chairman and General Superintendent was still a missionary, and the London Committee had the final say. Fifty years later, the Sierra Leone Synod requested the London Committee to appoint an acting chairman from among the African ministers of the District. In its Annual Letter, February 1, 1927, the London Committee replied:

> The present time or situation is not opportune for the making of this arrangement. The District has not yet extricated itself from a financial position which has given the greatest anxiety to the Committee, and has required of it again and again large measures of financial help. At the present time it will be difficult for one who is not a missionary sent out by the Committee to act in the double capacity of financial agent of the Committee and Chairman of the District.

On January 27, 1931, the Sierra Leone District Synod wrote to the Wesleyan Methodist Missionary Society in England, "It is a matter of regret, though not for complaint, that present conditions do not allow African representatives at Conference dealing with problems of Church and State affecting Africa and the African."

The year 1936 saw great friction between the Creole church leaders and the missionary chairman. The Synod requested his recall. The London Committee refused to do so and, moreover, discontinued the post of Assistant General Superintendent, occupied by a Creole, which had recently been established. The stated reasons were: (1) Regarding the decision not to recall the missionary, the highest court of the Methodist Church says so, and it cannot be questioned. (2) Regarding the discontinuing of the post of Assistant General Superintendent, the appointment was not serving the purpose for which it was intended and no man of suitable gifts and graces was available. The Church is not ready and united.

As a result, the District Synod "feels that the London Committee and the Conference have but very little, if any, sympathy with the aspirations of the African towards self-expression and self-determination" (Synod Minutes 1936).

One of the reasons for the decision of the London Committee was the lack of unity. The Creole churches were governed by Creoles, but the Chairman and General Superintendent was a missionary. He resided in Freetown and had authority over all the Church, both Creole and Mende. The rest of the missionaries were in the Mende Mission. The missionaries and Creoles disagreed with each other, and there was talk of dividing the Sierra Leone Synod into two districts — English and Mende. The London Committee rejected this proposal and proposed a closer cooperation, whereby the European missionaries would occasionally visit the Colony to preach.

In 1937 the Mende Mission Committee held its annual meeting separate from the Synod so it could be free from Creole domination, and by 1945 the two groups were still meeting separately. The Sierra Leone Synod objected to this because its members wanted the Mende Committee integrated into the Synod. But the Mende Committee refused because then there would have been little Mende representation, which would have meant Creole control. Ten years later (1955) a Mende Convention was held as an experiment to prepare the way for a possible Mende Area Council.

In 1956 the Reverend W. E. A. Pratt was nominated Acting Chairman during the furlough of the Chairman. In January, 1960, he became Chairman and General Superintendent. This position is annually nominated in the Synod and ratified in England. In 1966 the missionaries and Mende ministers of the Mende circuits were integrated into the whole Synod. In 1967 Sierra Leone became a separate Conference with two districts, Western and Provincial. The Reverend W. E. A. Pratt was elected President of the Conference.

## SUMMARY

1. The school approach succeeded among the Creoles but not among the tribespeople. It was and still is the policy to open a school at every station.

2. The Creoles were unsuccessful in planting tribal

churches, their efforts tending to result in Creole churches. The fear of Creole domination in the Mende Mission probably was justified.

3. The early mission policy of scattering missions all over the country in almost every tribe, sowed the seed of the Gospel but produced few results. Indications of ripeness were not followed up.

4. Concentration of evangelism among responsive people, with the goal of planting churches and with planned follow-up, produced people movements to Christ among the Creoles and Mende. It would probably have done so among the Limba.

# CHAPTER 7

# OTHER CREOLE CHURCHES

The Methodist and Anglican Churches are the largest Churches among the Creoles. Four other Creole Churches should be mentioned.

## COUNTESS OF HUNTINGDON'S CONNEXION*

This Church entered Sierra Leone by way of some Settlers who had become members of the Connexion while in Nova Scotia (Groves 1954). They were led by three Negro preachers and made no attempts to establish relations with the Connexion in England. They were thus lost sight of until 1825.

In that year the Connexion in England received a letter from the leader of "A Religious Society in the Connexion of the Countess of Huntingdon" in Sierra Leone. Contact was made again in 1839 when two members of the Sierra Leone Society went to London and reported on their religious activities, stating their membership as 879 in five stations in the Colony. Through the years they began stations in the interior. In recent years these churches, including some educated tribal evangelists, were turned over to other Churches according to a comity agreement. Their churches were confined to the stations and they never succeeded in winning the village people. The statistics for the Connexion in Sierra Leone, according to the *World Christian Handbook,* are:

Countess of Huntingdon's Connexion

|  | 1925 | 1949 | 1952 | 1957 | 1962 |
|---|---|---|---|---|---|
| Places of Worship |  | 3 | 4 | 14 | 14 |

* All references to this Church in the sources I used refer to it as "Connexion." Therefore, I have retained this spelling.

|  | 1925 | 1949 | 1952 | 1957 | 1965 |
|---|---|---|---|---|---|
| Communicants or Full Members |  |  |  |  | 1200 |
| Total Christian Community | 1205 | 500 | 500 | 1200 | 2000 |
| Staff: |  |  |  |  |  |
| Ordained: Nat'l |  |  |  | 4 |  |
| Ordained: Foreign |  | 1 | 1 | 1 |  |
| Laymen: Nat'l |  | 3 | 4 | 6 | 12 |
|  |  |  |  | (incl. | ordained) |
| Laymen: Foreign |  |  |  |  |  |

## SIERRA LEONE BAPTIST UNION

Baptists were also among the Nova Scotians who settled in Sierra Leone in 1792. They built a church and permitted none but Creoles to worship with them. As a result their one church has remained small, ingrown, and stagnant to this day.

In 1961 a Baptist missionary from England, after surveying the situation, declared the church hopeless from the standpoint of its becoming a missionary church. Therefore, he made arrangements to begin new missionary work in an unevangelized chiefdom on the Guinean border.* He built a mission residence in Freetown to enable him to supervise both the Creole congregation and the new mission.

## WEST AFRICAN METHODIST CHURCH

This Church began as a split from the Nova Scotian Methodist Church in Rawdon Street. The Settler preachers tried to suppress the liberated Africans by refusing to let them preach from the pulpit. So the liberated African preachers, in 1844, started a Church of their own.

In 1859 they applied for admission into the United Methodist Church (an amalgamation of a number of Wesleyan groups who had seceded from the main body in England). English missionaries came out to superintend the work of the Creole pastors, who in many cases were sent to England for training. The missionaries also began a mission at Tikonko (see map on page 95). In 1931 four missionaries with ten

---

* Interview with Rev. Clifford Gill.

pastors used forty-two buildings for their services. The mission had six centers of work in the Colony and eleven along the railroad.

In 1932 or 1933 the United Methodists in England, and the churches or circuits of Bo, Tikonko, Moyamba, and Banana Islands, merged with the Wesleyan Methodists. But some of the Creole churches refused to join and formed themselves into the West African Methodist Church. They have no foreign connection. Their few Creole churches in the interior were begun by members who were Creole traders.*

## AFRICAN METHODIST EPISCOPAL CHURCH
### (American Negro)

This Church entered Sierra Leone in the late 1800s. In the 1890s its missionaries were working among the aborigines who were flooding into Freetown. Neither the Methodists nor the Anglicans had been successful in reaching these people. In 1965 this denomination had four churches and one outstation in Freetown, and two churches in the provinces — all Creole. They had a school in Port Loko, but it closed and reopened under Roman Catholic management. They are now trying to reopen in Port Loko. No foreign personnel or funds are used and no foreigners are received except the Negro bishop, who was once an American, but is now a South African residing in Monrovia.**

* This history is a reconstruction based upon: *A Short History of Sierra Leone* (Fyfe 1962: 65); *Religion and Civilization in West Africa* (Cooksey and McLeish 1931: 113); Wesleyan Methodist Synod Minutes (1933), and an interview with Rev. I. S. T. Fewry, Superintendent of the Church.
** Interview with Conference Superintendent.

# CHAPTER 8

# THE CREOLE PROBLEM:
# IN RETROSPECT AND PROSPECT

## SPIRITUAL STATE

To the early Creoles (Settlers and liberated Africans), as to the Israelites of old, God was a* living reality. They had known physical bondage and had been liberated and brought over to their promised land. They had known spiritual bondage, and through Christ had been released to enjoy fellowship with God. They desired that others should be free, and helped lead the new arrivals of liberated Africans to Christ. Many returned to their homelands, such as Yorubaland in Nigeria, and Gold Coast (now Ghana), to tell the good news of Christ and civilization.

But the Creoles, as they became Christian and more literate, came to regard themselves as a people of God set apart from the original natives of Sierra Leone. S. A. J. Pratt, a Creole and active layman of the Sierra Leone Church (Anglican), says,

> The Canaanitish Timnes, and other indigenous tribesmen raided them now and again, but God and British guns always preserved the little band from extermination. Missionaries supplied them with spiritual, cultural and material food. The Creoles had education; they clung tenaciously to a mid-Victorian type of western culture and Christianity.... Unfortunately they quickly developed a spirit of patronizing superiority toward the indigenous tribesmen who formed and still form the great majority of the population of Sierra Leone (1956:154-155).

This spirit of patronizing superiority toward the common people, who form the great bulk of the population everywhere, is one of the problems of the Church in many lands. Those

105

who by virtue of education and redemption achieve position in society and become ministers, landowners, teachers, government officials, and the like, become culturally far removed from the humble people of the villages. They then become unable either to transmit Christianity among the common people or to administer a Church which will spread greatly. The Creole problem in Sierra Leone is a clear example of a problem which, in greater or lesser measure, adversely affects the growth of the Church everywhere. For example, Joseph Wold in his study of Liberia (1967) shows that the Americo-Liberians have also failed to communicate the Gospel to the general populace.

In the early period of missionary work in Sierra Leone the missionaries had high hopes of using the Creoles as missionaries for the spread of the Gospel throughout Africa, including Sierra Leone. The success of Creole missionaries among their own people in their homelands encouraged these hopes. Thus encouraged, the Church Missionary Society in 1860 turned over the colony churches to the Creoles, forming the Sierra Leone Native Pastorate, and pressed on into the hinterland of Sierra Leone. When missions among the tribes were established, these were turned over to the Creoles, the last being Falaba in 1907. The Methodist Mission experienced the same hopes and adopted the same pattern with its Creole Church. But gradually the missionary societies became disillusioned with the idea of Creoles evangelizing Sierra Leone. The Church Missionary Society withdrew, and the Methodist Missionary Society plunged ahead to evangelize the Mende, but without using Creole helpers.

The problem of maintaining a vital Christian faith among second generation Christians and their descendants is universal. Unless the Church constantly seeks to bring the children of Christians to a personal commitment of life to Christ, the churches drift into nominalism, formalism, or neopaganism. This has happened to the Creole Churches. Mr. Pratt describes the situation well:

> Christianity is a living religion, but the average Creole Christian does not seem to realise this. To him it is merely a world movement with a base in Sierra Leone, of which he is a member. This local base has meeting places or churches

which he attends regularly clad in his Sunday best, and where he goes through a set ritual in a parrot-like manner. He pays his church dues not so much from motives of charity or to assist in the propagation of the Gospel, but mainly to maintain his membership in this movement so that at his death he will be taken into Church for the first part of the Christian Burial Service. Since the churching of his corpse is his main reason for being a member in any particular church, he pays, if anything, only the minimum subscriptions due. Of course, being a professing Christian he is recognised as a respectable man (for isn't Christianity the religion of the State and of Great Britain?). In the Law Courts he can take his oath on a Bible instead of on a native "medicine." And last, but not least, he can in Christianity satisfy his thirst for ostentation during the Christian festivals, the celebration of Holy Matrimony, Holy Baptism, the Burial of the Dead, and Memorial Services. Outside of this his Christian witness is negligible.

How did this false conception of Christianity arise? It is axiomatic that all Creoles now living were born into a Christian home and were baptized in infancy — conversion plays very little part in bringing them to Christianity. English is not the mother tongue of the Creole: he speaks *Krio,* ... More often than not, as an infant, even before he can understand any English, he is taught to recite parrot-like the Lord's Prayer, the Creed, the Ten Commandments, a number of collects, hymns, psalms, etc. ... For the great majority of the Creoles, singing hymns and psalms, reading passages from the Bible, or saying set prayers in English involves a continuous process of mental effort in translating English into Krio. It is small wonder, then, that many follow the line of least resistance, and that the teachings of Christianity become an artificial part of their daily lives.

Something has to fill this vacuum of Christian living — the usual deadly sins see to that. What is sad is that some of this vacuum is filled with practices introduced by the "theists" [animists] from the hinterland, namely, the worship of the "good devils" [charms, juju]; in other words, idolatry is cultivated as a means of obtaining power, riches, honour, etc. ... [The Creoles'] skin-deep Christianity does not afford them sufficient strength to withstand the wiles of these "good devils." ... [So] the church grows poorer in faith and in resources, the "medicine man" grows richer and richer, and the Creole no longer enjoys spiritual peace of mind (1956:157-159).

Mr. Pratt then weighs the leadership of the Creoles, and finds them sadly wanting. There are, however, Mr. Pratt continues, "a few educated leaders who continue to be effective church members and to make their Christian witness at work and at leisure. They are not infrequently given such nicknames as Holy So-and-So, Prophet So-and-So. . . ."

Mr. Pratt paints a very depressing picture. He wrote in 1956, but the picture has not changed much since them. Raymond S. Foster (lately chaplain of Fourah Bay College, the University College of Sierra Leone, and examining chaplain to the Bishop of Sierra Leone) has written a contemporary study (1961) of the Sierra Leone Church, and shows that the Creoles are not wholly responsible for their present plight. A good share of the blame lies with the policy of the Church Missionary Society. To support this contention he quotes from Bishop Stephen Neill:

> Sierra Leone suffered from one of those premature and ill-considered attempts to create an independent Church. . . . As early as 1860 the Church Missionary Society brought into existence the Native Church Council, placing responsibility for the congregations in the hands of the African clergy, and reducing the missionary staff almost to vanishing point. The theory, of course, was that the Christians of the Colony area would gradually spread out into the interior and bring the Gospel to their African brethren. What happened, as ought to have been foreseen, was exactly the opposite (1957:166).

## DEVOLUTION

Neill is somewhat hasty in his judgment. The naiveté of the Society lay not in the formation of the Sierra Leone Native Pastorate in 1860, but in the continued turning over of missions to the Sierra Leone Church Missions, because by 1907 the Society should have seen that the Creole missionaries were establishing Creole missions. The Society ought not to have withdrawn until it had formed a Sierra Leone Tribal Pastorate serving truly tribal churches.

I asked earlier whether it was good strategy for the Church

Missionary Society to turn its entire work over to the Sierra Leone Church. Many mission boards and missionary societies advocate the policy of mission devolution, that is, the missionary should plant mission stations, institutions, and churches, and as soon as possible (the sooner, the better) he should turn them over — devolve the authority — to indigenous leaders and henceforth work through them, submitting to all their decisions. One of the beliefs supporting this policy is: Once the nationals are in charge of the Church, evangelization of their country will naturally accelerate. Ideally the policy ought to work; in practice, it is often wishful thinking. And because the mission board acts as though it were true, discipling the people often remains slow, slows down, or stops.

Bishop Stephen Neill asks a penetrating question which every mission board — and emerging national leadership — ought to ask when devolution is being considered, or after it already has taken place: But what is to happen, if a younger Church fails to rise to the heights of its responsibilities, and to take the initiative in setting evangelistic work in motion? Bishop Neill recognizes the problems involved but does not hesitate to speak clearly what he believes to be the mind of God:

> ... younger Church leaders sometimes give the impression that they would rather their fellow-countrymen died as heathens than that they should be brought to the knowledge of Christ by Christians from the West. If such a situation is reached, then there is nothing for it but for the older Churches to rebel. A dictatorship of the younger Churches is no better than a dictatorship of the missionary societies. Partnership is not a human alliance for mutual convenience, it is *partnership in obedience* to the command of Christ to preach the Gospel to every creature. If this obedience is lacking on one side or the other, the partnership would seem to lack a valid foundation. The world situation is changing so rapidly that opportunities are being lost every day. If an older Church seems to hear the clear call to evangelize, it may be necessary that it should go forward, leaving the younger Church to follow when it is sufficiently awake itself to hear the call (1957).

These remarks apply to Sierra Leone as well as to some other young Churches. The Methodists acted upon this answer by refusing to be tied to the Creole Church. But what about the Sierra Leone Church? Should the Church Missionary Society (1) re-establish mission work in the hinterland and forget the Sierra Leone Church; (2) re-enter, working through the Creole Church, or (3) leave the evangelization of Sierra Leone to the other missionary bodies?

Raymond Foster (1961:48-52) advocates the second solution. He asks that missionaries from the Anglican Communion of other countries around the world come and help, thus overcoming suspicions of Great Britain as the former colonial power. He recommends expatriate staff to strengthen the Creole churches, and additional staff to begin tribal work. There would be no problem of conflicting comity agreements because much of Sierra Leone is not being evangelized.

## COMMUNITY APPROACH FAILS

The method of evangelism Mr. Foster recommends is the community approach, in which individual converts are taken out of their pagan collective communities to form a new Christian collective community. He derives the pattern for this approach from (a) the experiment of the Church Missionary Society at Port Loko (1956-1959), (b) the book *What Is Evangelism?* by Douglas Webster, and (c) the Holy Cross Mission (Episcopal) in Liberia.

(a) The Church Missionary Society experiment at Port Loko used the traditional triad approach of education, medicine, and evangelism. A secondary school was built. A mobile medical van staffed by two nursing sisters, a priest, and his wife (a qualified nurse) sought to serve the village around Port Loko (there is a government hospital at Port Loko). This missionary staff was added to the resident Anglican priest at Port Loko (himself a Temne). Illness among the missionaries brought the experiment to a close. Foster does not say whether any tribesmen were converted or brought into the Church.

(b) Quoting extensively from *What Is Evangelism?*, Foster states his meaning of the community approach.

> Now, the Temne are not only Africans, they are also Muslims, in the main. A mission to the Temne thus demands special preparations. It is the conviction of the writer that the

only effective way of presenting the Christian Message under these circumstances is by a *Community*. "In Africa and Asia," writes Douglas Webster, "a collective society is the norm, though as a result of western education a few 'individuals' are emerging and breaking free from the bonds of the collective. . . . The chief mark of this type of society is the reluctance of the individual to act independently of the tribe or the group." Thus "the message proclaimed must become a reality in the life of the Church. The Christian fellowship has to demonstrate the dynamic of the Gospel before the eyes of on-looking groups and individuals": indeed, "may it not be that the best way of evangelizing these 'collectives' is by a Christian collective?" There must be a "base" from which the Christian mission can "go out," and into which the individual or the tribal group can "come in." The very best illustration of this is to be seen at Bolahun in Liberia, where the Holy Cross Fathers and the Holy Name Sisters have gradually expanded their community to include a new entirely Christian village, and from which the Christian message has radiated like the spokes of a wheel (1961).

This quotation shows a philosophy or policy of mission which is widespread but which does not win peoples for Christ. Instead, it often yields a small Christian community which is socially dislocated, highly civilized, heavily dependent on foreign mission resources, and as ineffective in winning tribespeople as Creoles are.

(c) Joseph C. Wold (1968), a Lutheran missionary in Liberia, discusses the Holy Cross Mission and shows how its community approach with much good mission work has failed to harvest the ripe fields.

Webster draws wrong conclusions from his ideas about tribal collective society. A collective society is won to Christ by approaching it as a unit. The method of approach is discussed in later chapters. A "Christian collective," on the other hand, grows by extracting and uprooting individuals one by one from the collective tribal society and transplanting them into itself. This cannot win peoples to Christ. The people movement approach disciples the collective tribal society and thereby produces a Christian tribal society, a society which is truly indigenous and capable of spontaneous expansion.

If the Sierra Leone Church, or any other Creole Church, desires to begin missionary work among tribal people, it must send out Creole or tribal missionaries who are willing both to become tribal in their outlook and to plant churches without Creole domination or orientation. In this situation the Creole is as much a foreigner as the European missionary, and his mission is cross-cultural.

# CHAPTER 9

# THE METHODIST MENDE CHURCH

The Mende Mission began in 1900 at Bandajuma. By 1922 the Missionary Society had decided to concentrate all its efforts among the Mende. Today the Methodists have churches in three separate areas of Mendeland: Sumbuya (Lower Mende), Tikonko (Lower Mende), and Segbwema-Bandajuma (Upper Mende). See the comity map on page 71. The graphs on page 114 comparing these three areas show the great difference in growth rates.

## SUMBUYA CIRCUIT

Until 1930 Sumbuya Circuit growth in members and catechumens bears marked resemblance to the Bandajuma graph of growth. The number of adult baptized members grew slowly and steadily (except for the drop in 1929) until the peak was reached in 1934 of 347 members in thirty-nine places of worship. Thereafter, the membership decreased until 1952, when eighty-eight members were scattered among twenty-one places of worship.

In 1951 a team sought to discover why this circuit was failing, and the following year reported its findings and recommendations at the annual meeting of the Synod. The report summarized the history of the circuit, stating that it began among settlers with services conducted in English, and became quite strong financially. But the persons in charge confined themselves largely to pastoral work among the Christians and did little itinerating or evangelism. When most of the settlers moved out, the church declined.

The report stated concerning the 1952 status of the circuit:

113

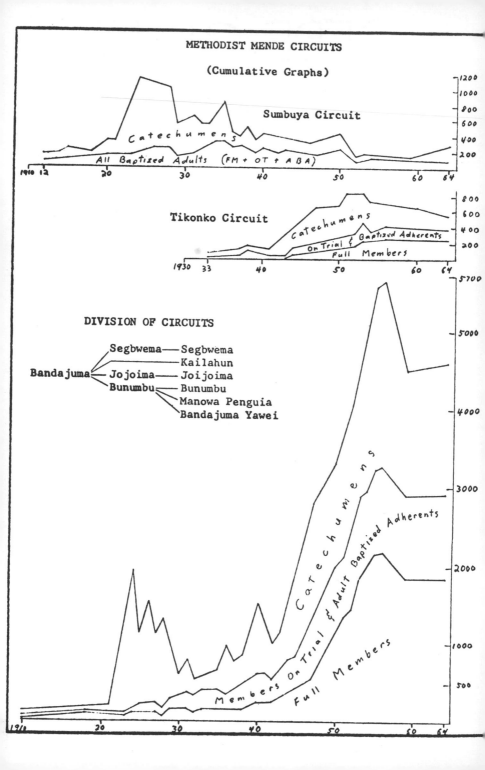

# METHODIST MENDE CIRCUITS

## (Cumulative Graphs)

Sumbuya Circuit

Catechumens

All Baptized Adults (FM + OT + ABA)

1910 12    20    30    40    50    60   64

1200 1000 800 600 400 200

Tikonko Circuit

Catechumens

On Trial & Baptized Adherents

Full Members

1930 33    40    50    60   64

800 600 400 200

### DIVISION OF CIRCUITS

Segbwema ——— Segbwema
               Kailahun
Bandajuma —— Jojoima ——— Joijoima
        Bunumbu —— Bunumbu
               Manowa Penguia
           Bandajuma Yawei

Catechumens

Members On Trial & Adult Baptized Adherents

Full Members

1910    20    30    40    50    60   64

5700 5000 4000 3000 2000 1000 500

Morale is low, and the "Mission" is looked to for nearly everything. There seems to be a low standard of personal morality and conduct throughout most of the area. Leadership, and a sense of belonging to a wider Christian community seems to have been lacking. Some places occupied are isolated units rather than centers from which groups of villages could be visited. There is no membership roll. Many people said that no Class Tickets had been distributed for several years. Some that we met, claiming to be leaders in the church, were polygamists and could not now be Members. The Circuit is widely scattered, with large gaps of unoccupied territory. But *there are possibilities of revival if a vernacular policy is pursued and the young life in the schools can be brought into a vernacular church.* This is our conviction. (Italics mine.)

Eight of the eleven stations were visited. (Another two had been turned over to the adjacent United Brethren in Christ Church according to a comity arrangement.)

This is a typical, but tragic, story. It reveals again the extreme difficulty English-speaking churches face if they hope to win the tribespeople. The solution advocated is half right — "There are possibilities of revival if a vernacular policy is pursued. . . ." However, "the young life in the schools" do not like being in a vernacular church. If the tribespeople are to be won, the school must be left to operate within its own realm. The leaders of the vernacular churches must be vernacular themselves, with guidance from trained leaders who are fully sympathetic with the indigenous way of life.

Noticeably absent from the report is an analysis of statistical data. The growth picture on the graph (page 114) cries for explanation. Who were the 957 catechumens in 1924? Where did they live? If it is true that the minister or catechist did only pastoral work, who enrolled them? Why were they not prepared for baptism and brought into the Church of Christ — into the Kingdom of God? The records of the individual churches or societies of the circuit, if they are still extant, ought to be studied to answer these questions. It appears from the overall circuit statistics that *God prepared a field, making it ready for harvest, and the laborers did not gather the harvest in!* Most of those catechumens of 1924, over forty years ago, are now dead and lost forever! How much the salvation of men and women depends upon the activities and right decisions of God's servants!

## TIKONKO CIRCUIT

This circuit came under Methodist jurisdiction in 1933 after the merger with the (British) United Methodists. In 1934 eleven full members, two members on trial, and sixty-three catechumens worshipped in twenty-seven preaching places. The full membership did not rise above seventeen until 1944, ten years later. One wonders what was being done with the catechumens. Perhaps they were school children. The records do not say.

A literacy campaign, in accordance with Methodist practice, was launched in Tikonko Circuit, yielding a high rate of literacy among the Christians. This should have produced a growing church. After slow growth for a decade (1944-1954), and slower growth for three years, growth has stopped. The Methodists need to find the reason for this and try new strategy to win the people to Christ. The rise in catechumens from 1941 to 1951 probably indicates ripeness. However, catechumens become the growing edge of the Church only if they are trained, baptized, and brought into full membership. The three jumps in the "Members on Trial" line corresponds with larger numbers of catechumens being baptized.

The people may yet be ripe, and many respond if right methods are used.

## BANDAJUMA CIRCUIT

Hardly any growth occurred in this circuit until 1923, the year the Wesleyan Methodist Missionary Society decided to concentrate its efforts in this area. That year three separate circuits were organized, each bearing a different name from the original. The plans for advance, submitted by the Synod to headquarters in London in a letter dated January 27, 1923, were:

1. That we occupy the following Chiefdoms, headquarters being at: Jojoima, Daru, Jaluahun-Segbwema, Bunumbu and Bandajuma.

2. That the following activities be put into operation:

    a. An elementary Boys' Boarding School in each Chiefdom

    b. A Central Boarding School for boys and a Training Institution to be placed in Bunumbu

    c. A Girls' Boarding School to be placed in Daru

    d. A Dispensary in each Chiefdom with a Central Medical Store placed at Segbwema

    (N.B. In order to carry out this program one additional European Missionary, two Wesley Deaconesses, and one Nurse will be necessary. These additions to the staff we consider to be our minimum requirements.)

3. That the following buildings be erected without delay:

    a. A new Mission House in Segbwema

    b. A new Mission House in Bunumbu

    c. A new Mission House for the Deaconesses at Daru

    d. A new Church in Segbwema.

The triad approach of education, medicine, and evangelism was the method chosen to win the people. The graphs on page 118 show its relative success. Jojoima, after a good start, faded to a static church. (The people movement map on page 119 shows Jojoima without a circuit boundary, to avoid an illusion of occupied territory.) The area is strongly influenced by Islam, and social pressure is against Christianity. The missionaries feel that a mere decision to become a Christian indicates depth, so anyone who shows interest in Christ is baptized and brought into full membership as quickly as possible in order to avoid discouragements.

## SEGBWEMA CIRCUIT

Segbwema, a trading center on the railroad, became the center of "the plan for advance." The mission built a large cement block church and a hospital on opposite hills. Today there are three separate mission compounds within the town limits: (1) the circuit superintendent mission compound, including a primary school and church, (2) the hospital compound, and (3) a boys' secondary boarding school, opened in 1965. Within the circuit, four miles from Segbwema, is another mission compound. This is divided into three sections, each with its own missionary residences: (1) a vernacular

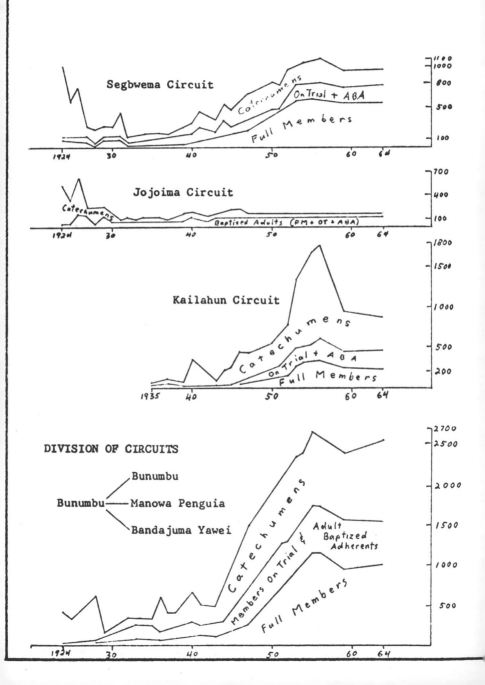

# METHODIST MENDE CIRCUITS

## (Cumulative Graphs)

Segbwema Circuit

Catechumens
On Trial + ABA
Full Members

1924    30    40    50    60    64

1100
1000
800
500
100

Jojoima Circuit

Catechumens
Baptized Adults (FM + OT + ABA)

1924    30    40    50    60    64

700
400
100

Kailahun Circuit

Catechumens
On Trial + ABA
Full Members

1935    40    50    60    64

1800
1500
1000
500
200

DIVISION OF CIRCUITS

Bunumbu —— Manowa Penguia
Bandajuma Yawei

Bunumbu

Catechumens
Members On Trial & Adult Baptized Adherents
Full Members

1924    30    40    50    60    64

2700
2500
2000
1500
1000
500

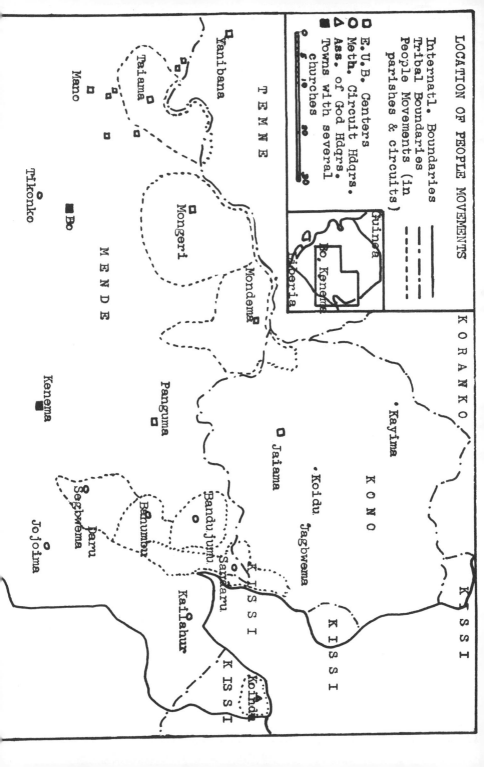

LOCATION OF PEOPLE MOVEMENTS

Internatl. Boundaries
Tribal Boundaries
People Movements (in
  parishes & circuits)

□ E.U.B. Centers
○ Meth. Circuit Hdqrs.
▲ Ass. of God Hdqrs.
■ Towns with several
  churches

Guinea

Bo, Kenema

Liberia

TEMME

Yanibana

Taiama

Mano

Mongeri

Tikonko

Bo

MENDE

Mondema

Panguma

Kenema

Kayima

Koidu
Jagbwema

Jaiama

KONO

Behumbu

Bandujuma

Samaaru

Daru
Segbwema

Jojoima

Kailahun

KISSI

Koindu

KISSI

KORANKO

KISSI

KISSI

Women's Training Centre, (2) a secondary boarding school for girls, and (3) a vernacular Bible School.

According to the current plan, one missionary is appointed as circuit superintendent, responsible for church life and primary school management in the circuit, and all others are assigned to medical and educational activities. The Mende Bible School near Segbwema served all the Mende circuits until its closing in 1965 for lack of staff, and was directly involved in the growth of the Church. The vernacular Women's Training Centre still serves the Mende circuits and is helping it to train laywomen. The great majority of converts and local church leaders, including catechists, do not know English. The program of the Mende Bible School has been held partly responsible for this, so during its closure the program is being reevaluated.

The primary and secondary schools do not directly serve the local churches because most children who become literate do not remain in the villages. A few become teachers and catechists, but most leave this "remote" area and seek employment in larger towns such as Kenema, Bo, or Freetown. However, the school system does serve the country as a whole, producing many Christian leaders who will help make Sierra Leone a nation which operates on Christian principles.

The Methodist Church, in cooperation with the other member Churches of the United Christian Council of Sierra Leone, ought to conduct a thorough survey to see what percentage of children become active church members after leaving church-managed schools. Only thus can the Churches know what Christian effect the school system is having upon the intelligentsia of the nation. This study shows that the school approach is not winning the nonliterate tribespeople. But to what extent has it won the children after they have finished school?

Neither do the maternity clinics, dispensaries, and hospitals directly help local churches grow, although they provide needed medical assistance and exhibit God's love. This will be discussed further under Benevolences in the next chapter.

We now turn to the growth of the Church in Segbwema Circuit. The graph of the Bandajuma circuits on page 114 shows a gain of 1665 catechumens from 1921 to 1924, followed by a net* loss of 1366 by 1930. These years mark the beginning of the concentrated effort among the Mende. The records locate the gains and losses (see the circuit graphs on page 118) but do not reveal the cause.

Segbwema Circuit (see map on page 119) began in 1924 with 880 catechumens and 123 members, with most of the members probably Creole traders in Segbwema and Daru. When membership growth came in 1939, it was slow. It stopped after fifteen years and has not grown for a decade. In 1964 the membership was 789, plus 190 catechumens, or 6.6 per cent of the adult (fifteen years and older) population. Fourteen thousand adults have yet to commit themselves to Christ in the Jaluahun Chiefdom (Segbwema). The map on page 119 locates the circuit, within which were thirty-four churches in 1959.

## KAILAHUN CIRCUIT

Kailahun Circuit began later than the others on the graph (page 118). The number of catechumens increased in 1940, but very few became members. The rise in membership corresponds directly with the number of adults baptized in any year. As in Segbwema Circuit, after 1956 the membership declined. Note again the peak of Kailahun Circuit on the graph. The large number of catechumens, which were steadily being enrolled up until 1956 — 1171 of them — were not baptized and brought into responsible membership in the Church. The Methodist Church ought to inquire what happened to them. Were they school children? Were stiffer rules introduced to make sure converts were "sincere" before they were permitted to continue as catechumens? Was there a migration away from the area? It is significant that *all three circuits with growing churches stopped and declined at the same time.*

## MANOWA-PENGUIA CIRCUIT**

Bunumbu Circuit divided, and divided again, as it grew

* From 1924 to 1930 there was a gain of 133 members and a loss of 1499 catechumens.
** I am indebted to the Rev. Roger Smith and the Rev. Sidney Groves for much of the information in this section.

too large to be supervised by one minister. The growing edge at present is in Manowa-Penguia Circuit with headquarters at Sandaru. Christianity is moving north, up the valley, to include the Kissi and Kono (see the people movement map on page 119). A mission station was opened at Sandaru (the paramount chief town of Penguia Chiefdom) because the people there were ripe for harvest. Synod minutes of 1952 state that after the paramount chief resigned, a missionary went to the chiefdom (about 1951) and found "groups of people in village after village, anxious to join the Church, and asking to be taught the Christian way of life. He was unable to cover all the area, but on that one visit 144 people were enrolled as catechumens: all won by the faithful witness of a lone Christian who has been living for a few years in that Chiefdom."

Manowa-Penguia Circuit is organized for numerical and spiritual growth in the way revealed in the table on the following page. The circuit is divided into seven sections, each with a full-time paid lay catechist in charge. This division usually corresponds with the political division of the chiefdom. Six of the section towns, including the paramount chief town, have primary schools. The responsibility of the catechist is to conduct Sunday services in the section town where he is stationed and to hold class meetings once a week in each of the village churches in the section. At the close of a class meeting the catechist reads the roll from the class record book, at which time each Christian (inquirer,* catechumen, and member**) announces his presence and pays his class dues. The catechist is also responsible for teaching the catechism class in each village. Should a catechist have too many villages for all to be visited each week, those farther away receive fewer visits.

The class leaders and local preachers are voluntary lay workers, although some are school teachers. Village churches of the section are called classes and are comparable to the classes of the larger Creole churches. Almost every class has a local preacher whose responsibility is to conduct the other

---

* "Inquirer" is a person who shows interest in Christianity but has not yet been enrolled as a catechumen.

** "Member" comprises members on trial, adult baptized adherents, and full members.

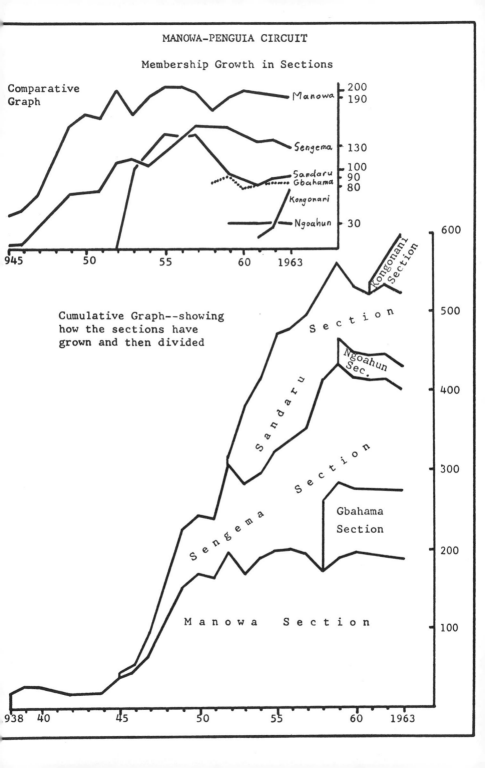

MANOWA-PENGUIA CIRCUIT

Membership Growth in Sections

Comparative
Graph

Manowa — 200
190

Sengema — 130

Sandaru — 100
Gbahama — 90
80

Kongonani

Ngoahun — 30

945    50    55    60    1963

Cumulative Graph--showing
how the sections have
grown and then divided

Kongonani Section

Section

Ngoahun Sec.

Sandaru

Sengema    Section

Gbahama
Section

Manowa    Section

600

500

400

300

200

100

938  40    45    50    55    60    1963

services of the week (other than the one the catechist conducts). He does not record attendance or receive offerings.

All offerings (class dues) and class record books are brought monthly by the catechists to the circuit superintendent. The money goes into the circuit fund from which the catechists are paid. In the monthly meeting the circuit superintendent conducts a Bible study and examines the class record books. He regularly visits each class to exhort, receive inquirers into catechumen status, determine who are ready for baptism and for full membership, and call the names of those who are regularly absent to warn them. He also baptizes and gives communion, and he is the school manager for the primary schools. Each class (village church) in reality is a church unto itself, for its members do not meet at a center or mother church for larger group fellowship and worship. Each village church with communicant members receives communion at least once a year, but the section town churches and nearby village churches receive it more often.

A person desiring to become a full member first becomes an *inquirer* by attending church regularly. After he has been "listening" from one to six months, if he wishes to become a *catechumen,* he will attend a short course in which he will learn that a Christian must

(1) leave his old ways, such as
    (a) spirit worship, sacrifice;
    (b) Islamic practices, and
    (c) immoral ways: adultery, drunkenness, abusive language, making oaths on "medicine," and polygamy, and
(2) make a sincere promise at a decision service to
    (a) leave these things behind and
    (b) follow Jesus, learn His ways, and give thank offerings and money to God for His work.

The Methodists have a vernacular (Mende) catechism which is divided into three parts: (1) general doctrine about God, Christ, and salvation; (2) church doctrine about the meaning of the Church, its sacraments, and the duties of church members, and (3) the life of Jesus in outline form. The catechumen preparing himself for baptism must master the first and third parts. This may take from one to three years. After he completes the course he is baptized and becomes a *member on trial*. He remains on trial for about six to nine months, in which time he studies part two of the catechism. If he lapses by taking a second wife or breaking some other church law he becomes an *adult baptized adherent* and cannot become a full member. But if he perseveres and finishes the course, and his walk of life and his church attendance are satisfactory, he becomes a full member. As a full member he may receive communion and hold church office.

A full member desiring to become a local preacher must first conduct services in the village as a *local preacher on trial*. Then the circuit superintendent arranges for him to take a correspondence course, which comes from Kajola Institute, Nigeria, is translated into Mende, and is administered by someone designated by the Synod. When the candidate finishes the course, after three years or more, he gets a certificate showing he is a local preacher. If a local preacher (on trial or certificated) is doing well and there is an opening, he is appointed as a catechist on a salary of about Le 5 (5 Leones, or £2.10.0, or $7) per month.

The structure and plan for church growth is clear and methodical and was used in all the circuits. Its success is related to the readiness of the people within a circuit to be harvested into the Kingdom of God. Around Jojoima and Sumbuya it failed. In the circuits of Tikonko, Segbwema, and Kailahun it had moderate success, and then growth stopped. The same is true of Bunumbu and Bandajuma.

It has had greater success in Manowa-Panguia Circuit, although not the success it could have had. The graphs on the following page show that the sections have stopped growing. The exception is Kongonani, which is still in its period of initial growth. Sukudu section (Kono), which began in 1962, is not shown because in 1963 it had only one member, but forty-nine catechumens.

Many of the villages are small, each comprising one extended family, some with fifty adults or more and some with as few as thirteen adults in five houses.

Christianity preceded Islam in many of the villages, and in some Islam has not yet come. Lalehun, a Kissi town on the river across from Guinea, had in 1964 twenty Muslims and forty-two adult Christians out of a population of 230 (an estimate based on 112 male taxpayers). Most of the Christians belong to one extended family. Thirty-five had become Christian since 1961, twenty-one of them after choosing between Christ and Mohammed. Only four had been baptized and none

## METHODIST CHURCH

### Manowa-Penguia Circuit

### November 1964

| Section | Churches | Other Buildings Used for Worship | Catechists | Voluntary Workers | | Member-ship | | Adult Baptized Adherents | Catechumens | Baptisms in 1964 | Total Baptized |
|---|---|---|---|---|---|---|---|---|---|---|---|
| | | | | Local Preachers | Class Leaders | Full Members | On Trial | | | | |
| Manowa | 3 | 4 | 1 | 11 | 3 | 109 | 39 | 34 | 58 | 0 | 18. |
| Gbahama | 4 | 7 | 1 | 7 | 2 | 59 | 9 | 10 | 38 | 0 | 7. |
| Sengema | 3 | 6 | 1 | 6 | 3 | 77 | 42 | 5 | 99 | 0 | 12. |
| Sandaru | 4 | 4 | 1 | 7 | 2 | 49 | 41 | 3 | 71 | 0 | 9. |
| Ngaahun | 5 | 2 | 1 | 2 | 6 | 16 | 55 | 0 | 110 | 0 | 7. |
| Kongonani | 2 | 8 | 1 | 4 | 2 | 21 | 5 | 1 | 156 | 0 | 2. |
| Sukudu | 1 | 9 | 1 | 1 | 0 | 2 | 0 | 0 | 83 | 0 | . |
| Totals | 22 | 40 | 7 | 38 | 18 | 333 | 191 | 53 | 615 | 0 | 57. |

was receiving instruction for baptism. The local preacher was the schoolteacher.

Sukudu is the newly formed Kono section, separated from Kongonani. In 1963, 280 were ready to be enrolled as catechumens. By the end of the year only forty-nine had been enrolled.

The catechumen and membership enrollments for the whole circuit were:

MANOWA-PENGUIA CIRCUIT

| Year | Number of Catechumens | Increase or Decrease | Number of Members | Increase or Decrease |
|------|------------|----------|----------|----------|
| 1961 | 460 |  | 538 |  |
| 1962 | 495 | +35 | 565 | +27 |
| 1963 | 519 | +24 | 602 | +37 |
| 1964 | 519 | 00 | 600 | - 2 |

The evidence clearly shows that the discipling of the people is *not* keeping pace with their readiness to become Christian. The Methodist Mende circuit superintendents, the Sierra Leone Conference, and the London Committee should note this and rectify the situation.

## BAPTISMAL REQUIREMENTS

Why are the people not being harvested in accordance with their readiness? At Jojoima, when anyone shows interest in Christ, he is baptized and brought into full membership as quickly as possible. In the more ripe circuits, great care is taken lest someone become a member who is merely following the tide of group acceptance. This attitude is based on the commonly held, yet false assumption that decisions against social pressure are sincere while those with social pressure are suspect; and that the former make sounder, better quality Christians.

On the contrary, the reverse is more likely to be true. Many (but by no means all) who decide to become Christian against social pressure are misfits in their societies and are using Christianity as an opportunity to rebel. By becoming Christian, they harden the opposition against Christianity and give it the stigma of being a religion of misfits. On the other hand, many (but not all) who decide to become Christian at the same time as others are sincere in their decisions and, further-more, have the advantage of a Christian fellowship to enable them to grow stronger in the faith.

We cannot accurately discern the motives of people turn-ing to Christ. Even if we could, we would be unable to pre-dict what kind of Christian a convert will become. The reason for becoming a Christian does not determine the quality of Christian life, but the follow-up and spiritual care the convert receives after coming into the Church do. The person influenced by his family or village to become Christian is much more likely to receive the spiritual care and social support necessary to become strong than the person who becomes Christian in a hostile environment.

The problem the missionary or minister faces, then, is not to discover which Christians are sincere enough to be bap-tized and become full members, but rather to reap the harvest at the peak of interest, before the people turn cool. An ex-ample of this is Bishop Pickett's experience in Kenya.* After speaking to a group of three hundred Indians, he invited some to become Christian. In reply, one man arose and asked why the bishop invited only some to become Christian. Bishop Pickett then invited all the Indians. All three hundred, there-upon, declared their desire to become Christian and to be baptized. Pickett referred them to the priest in charge. But the priest, being cautious and not wanting to be hasty lest some would be baptized who were unworthy, baptized only fifteen — and the rest changed their minds.

Two problems are likely to arise when we select those whom we think are ready: (1) We are likely to get those who are agreeable to us, and (2) the larger group may turn against the selected persons and the total group is divided.

Eugene Nida, in his book *Message and Mission,* has stated the situation well. He points out that there are always a host of internal problems in the growth of Christian movements. One of them is the tendency to think that everything must be done at once according to some strict sequence:

When confronted with a dramatic response to the gospel,

* Donald A. McGavran, reporting an interview with Bishop Pickett, in a class lecture, February 21, 1966, at the School of World Mission — Institute of Church Growth, Fuller Theological Seminary.

there has often been a tendency for missionaries to think that everything must be taught to the people all at once, and that without thorough instruction no one should be permitted to "advance" to church membership. There is, of course, some sound reasoning in such caution, for in some situations the church has been packed by people whose motives were suspect and whose understanding was faulty. On the other hand, an even more tragic mistake is to try to do everything at once, or to insist that people who do not understand much of the content of the message must pass along by certain prescribed stages (like the order in Masonry) in order to be fully accredited believers, even though their loyalties have been won to Christ. As McGavran has pointed out so well [in *Bridges of God* (1955)], a distinction must be made between discipling and teaching. *One must make every effort to "process" the new converts as quickly as possible, while the fires of their new loyalties are burning brightly and their enthusiasm is sufficient to see them through some of the inevitable radical changes and adjustments.* It is quite true that in most people's movements illiteracy is high and Biblical knowledge is low. Nevertheless, such groups are usually stable, rooted in the indigenous culture — a natural bridge for communication to others — and have remarkable possibilities for growth, if within the first generation there has been dynamic and vigorous thrust in the direction of the church. *It is this crucial first impulse which must be carefully guarded and properly employed if the fullest results are to be realized* (1960: 147-148; italics mine).

This is not to say that there are to be no standards for admission to baptism and membership. It *is* to say that baptism and church membership are the *beginning* of the Christian life, *not the reward* for having proved oneself a good strong Christian. Baptism and church membership are part of the discipling process. Perfection (that is, growth in the Christlike life) begins there, and continues throughout the Christian's life as he is nurtured through worship, study, and fellowship.

What then ought the standards for admission to baptism and membership be? There must be some criterion whereby a minister can decide whether a person has truly repented, that is, has truly turned his back on the old way and has put his faith in Christ. That criterion will be discussed later. The emphasis at this point is the relationship of method to goal. In broad terms, the goal of all Churches and Missions is to win people to Christ. This goal is not easily attained. All the Creole Churches, for example, have this goal, but are doing little or nothing to achieve it.

## Typical Evangelism

Vague goals yield vague methods. The following is typical. A minister is assigned to a circuit, within which are catechists and school teachers. He preaches in the town church while the catechists preach in their churches and among the villages. Hopefully, as people listen they will become interested in the Gospel, begin to attend meetings regularly — or as regularly as the catechist comes to the village — and have their names recorded. After some weeks or months those who wish baptism receive special instruction. Those who persevere to the end are baptized and become members. Some catechumens, perhaps many, fail to attend regularly, gradually losing interest. Perhaps some, having more than one wife, are not eligible for baptism.

Gradually a few people here and there become church members, although never very many in any one village. Statistics are duly recorded (maybe) and sent on to be filed somewhere. Preachers continue itinerating and the people still listen, but no additional people attend the meetings. Large numbers of animists and Muslims continue as they are, and the Christians gradually lose members as some backslide.

The fault lies in lack of proper goals. If the goal is to win people to Christ and plant churches, definite plans must be laid to win whole families, whole villages, whole sections, whole chiefdoms to Christ. The goal should be whole social units. The emphasis in preaching and teaching should be such that the hearers, as they become interested in Christianity, will do all within their power to see that their whole families and villages, and families in other villages, turn to Christ.

Christianity is not only a religion for the individual, it is God's religion for society. Christ died that both the hearer and his family and social patterns might be saved. Definite plans, therefore, must be laid so that people may see salvation in its wider scope, and that social units, as units, might leave the old way with its ancestor supplications, witchcraft, sacrifices, and charms, and accept Jesus' way.

When a social unit, in whole or in part, turns to Christ, all its members should be enrolled as catechumens and continue witnessing to others. The length of training need not be long, but the essentials should be learned. Ardor in serving Christ rather than intellectual attainment should be the criterion for determining who is ready to be baptized. While their interest is high they should be baptized and brought into full membership. They will not be perfect. Some may be doing what white men have learned is sin. However, the participants may not consider them as sin. But, praise be to God, He does not require a person to be sinless *before* he turns to Him. God only requires that his heart be changed — converted — and that he desire to follow God through Christ. Baptism and membership are but the beginning of the Christian life. Perfection and a deeper understanding of sin will develop later.

Reception into full communicant membership should occur at the time of baptism. A person Christian enough to be baptized is Christian enough to receive communion. As members commune together their spiritual lives become strengthened. Many ministers err in considering communion a reward for being holy and good. Rather, communion is a reminder to ourselves and to the world of Christ's death for our sins and of His continued presence with us, for which we give thanks.

Eugene Nida, in his discussion of indigenous Christian movements (or people movements), speaks of their "cooling off."

> Once a Christian movement has reached its peak of expansion, instead of maintaining a high plateau of spiritual life and activity it normally tends to "cool off." Not that the people return to the same level of religious response as before the "revival" or "movement"; but they may well become "lukewarm" about the new faith (1960: 150).

Many ministers have noticed and bemoaned this tendency. But Nida says that nothing is essentially strange about this reaction, for it is typical of all human movements, religious or otherwise.

Some of the reasons he points out are: (1) lack of organization to effect common goals, so interest wanes; or too much organization, so that the momentum of the movement is exhausted to keep the organization running; (2) the Gospel becomes old and commonplace so that *faith* tends to become *creed,* and *creed* ends up as mere *recitation;* (3) the Gospel may lose its distinctiveness by syncretism with the old religion, and (4) the effect of those who are not within the movement. Developing number (4), Nida says,

> ... when a particular segment of society is simply outside the movement, for one reason or another, it has an effect upon the "temperature" inside, even though there is no special opposition. ... Thus to concentrate heavily upon one segment of the society, while neglecting the structure as a whole, means that the enthusiasm of that one segment may cool off rapidly when it returns to the larger setting (1960: 155).

Nida offers two essential techniques to reduce the cooling-off effect and to provide the movement with a continuing momentum as a means of increasing its drive and extending its influence. He states that (1) new information must be constantly supplied to the movement, and (2) new applications of this information must be found. For example, there needs to be continual training of leaders and laymen through training programs and Sunday School; and the Christians must continually apply the information learned to their lives, their social conditions, and to winning others.

The Methodists' excellent organizational system could implement the above plans of expansion and spiritual growth in winning whole villages — whole chiefdoms — to Christ. The many non-Christian pockets need winning.

> The growth of any movement is in direct proportion to the success of that movement in mobilizing its total membership for the propagation of its beliefs.

This is the axiom upon which the Evangelism in Depth movement bases its strategy. It is the axiom which every church leader and member must take seriously if the people are to be won. A revival is needed so that all Christians may participate in winning the rest of their families and villages to Christ. The Churches which do not have such an organization would do well to adapt it to their own church structures.

One type of leader the Methodists lack which would aid in growth, both spiritual and numerical, is the unpaid itinerator. This type of leader will be discussed later.

International boundaries usually become barriers which prevent missionaries from spreading Christianity to adjacent countries. However, missionaries should seek to cross such boundaries in order to reap the whole harvest of souls. Most of the Kissi tribe live in Guinea and Liberia. The small responsive pocket in Manowa-Penguia Circuit indicates that probably the Kissi across the river in Guinea are also responsive. Catechists could cross to preach in the villages. God has shown that the Kissi in that area are ripe for harvest. It is the responsibility of Churches and mission boards to send reapers into the harvest.

# CHAPTER 10

# THE EVANGELICAL UNITED BRETHREN CHURCH

This chapter discusses six aspects of the propagation of the Gospel which are met by missions and churches around the world, using cases from the Evangelical United Brethren Church as typical examples. These problems are dealt with topically except for the first section, which gives the historical setting.

*The School Approach* (page 137) shows how schools have been founded to win the tribespeople, but have tended to center efforts on education rather than on winning villagers to Christ.

*Organizational Structure and the Ministry* (page 142) illustrates the need for a two-level ordained ministry: one to meet the spiritual needs of the educated people in town churches and the other to meet the spiritual needs of the nonliterate populace in the villages.

*Money* (page 148) deals with the problem of self-support and whether evangelists ought to be sent by, paid by, and responsible to a central authority, e.g., Conference.

*Devolution* (page 152) shows how the transfer of authority from Mission to Church, which occurs as part of the school approach, tends to create a dictatorial type of leadership which prevents the maximum expansion of the Church, and suggests an "indigenous" approach which would give greater freedom and church expansion.

*Church Growth* (page 156) presents several case studies showing how the people of the land have been and may be won to Christ. The summary of this section begins on page 166.

*Benevolences* (page 167) illustrates how foreign mission

134

social service sometimes hinders the primary goal of discipling peoples and planting churches, and suggests how social service may be restructured so as to benefit the emerging Church and the general population.

Evangelical United Brethren readers will probably wish to study these sections carefully. Readers of other denominations may wish to study only the summaries of each. The section on *Church Growth* (page 156) may prove the most useful because it deals with methods of evangelism and church planting which have been successful in winning villagers to Christ.

## BEGINNINGS*

The Mission Board of the United Brethren in Christ (now Evangelical United Brethren), at its first annual session on June 1, 1854, appointed three missionaries to begin mission work in Africa. They landed at Freetown on February 26, 1855, and spent two years trying to locate a field in which to begin their work. They were assisted in their search by the American Missionary Association of New York, which had begun the Mende Mission fourteen years earlier. In March, 1857, Thomas Stephen Caulker, descendant on the paternal side of a conquering English slave trader, and the paramount chief at Shenge, was induced to give a one-hundred-year lease for about one hundred acres of land adjoining the town of Shenge (see comity map on page 71).

> On this beautiful location, one of the most healthful spots along this coast, the headquarters for our work was established. Here, finally, the mission home, the Rufus Clark and Wife Training School, the Flickinger Chapel, boys' home, parsonage, Eastborne, and minor buildings were erected, part of the land planted in coffee trees, and a part of it continuously farmed (Mills 1898: 74).

In 1875, the Women's Missionary Association (now Women's Society of Christian Service) of the United Brethren in Christ was organized, and they became co-workers with the General Board of Missions in "carrying forward the enterprise"

* The source of much of the historical information contained in this section is the book, *Mission Work in Sierra Leone, West Africa* (Mills 1898).

in Sierra Leone. They located their headquarters at Rotifunk in 1877.

> At this center of the work of the Woman's Missionary Association there is [1898] a chapel, high-school building, home for the missionaries, girls' home, boys' home, a workshop, and a storehouse — all good buildings of wood and stone. They had employed in this field, the first of May, 1898, eight Americans, two of whom were physicians, one a mechanic, and five were teachers or pastors; also eight native pastors and teachers. These were employed at twelve different circuits or stations. Some of these circuits included forty towns and villages where services were held, and new fields were being entered continually by these zealous workmen (Mills 1898: 77).

In 1883 the American Missionary Association turned over its Mende Mission to the United Brethren in Christ General Board of Missions.

> Their two chief stations were Good Hope, at Bonthe, where there was a good chapel, school-house, residence, and a tract of land now in the city of Bonthe; and Avery, where there was a good chapel, residence, sawmill, and a coffee farm; a farm at Kaw-Mendi (Commendi) and one at Mo-Tappan were included. . . . The American Missionary Association had become discouraged over the meager returns, and wishing to engage in mission work elsewhere, after an expenditure of $300,000 (so I was informed), and the death of many of their workmen they kindly transferred all their African interests to us (Mills 1898: 77-78).

Eighteen years passed (1857-75) before the first church was planted. Five years later the West African Conference was organized. The more rapid advance came after the arrival, in 1870, of the Reverend and Mrs. Joseph Gomer, American Negro missionaries. Under Gomer's influence the first convert of the mission, Thomas Tucker, made a fuller consecration of himself to God. Gomer pushed Tucker forward in religious services and influenced Chief Caulker to appoint Tucker as sub-chief over a large district. In 1883 Tucker became a preacher of the Gospel.

Bishop J. S. Mills (1898) summarized the progress of the mission:

From small beginnings, and after years of discouragement, the work suddenly sprang forward, wide revivals followed, and now [1898] over 6,000 souls have had their names placed on church records, most of whom, it is believed, are converted to God from their former heathenism. The work has spread from Shaingay [Shenge] in the west to Mongherri in the east; and from Rokell in the north to Bonthe in the south. Of course, the whole region is not occupied, but its conquest is under way.

Mills' map on page 138 shows the location of stations in 1898. Sixteen of the stations had farms of 100 to 160 acres each. These farms were given by the native chiefs as a contribution to the support of missions and schools. The farms, however, have never been fully utilized.

In 1898, during the Hut Tax War, two Evangelical United Brethren couples and three single lady missionaries were massacred at Rotifunk and Taiama, plus many teachers, catechists, and other Christians; and the buildings at the mission stations were destroyed. The hospital at Rotifunk is named in memory of the two women doctors who were slain — Miss Mary C. Archer and Miss Marietta Hatfield. After the war most of the buildings were rebuilt. The West African Conference Journals record the post-war expansion of the mission as follows:*

1909   Hangha opened.
1910   Pendembu opened (at the end of the railway and now in the Methodist comity area).
       Gambia opened (in Susuland, now in the American Wesleyan Methodist comity area).
       Jaiama in Konoland opened.
1920   Mongere reopened.
1926   Boajibu closed.
1933   Tabe reopened and four stations closed.

## THE SCHOOL APPROACH

More important than the mere opening of stations is the dynamics of growth — the philosophy and implementation of mission work. The Evangelical United Brethren used, and still use, the school approach. All the stations had schools, whether

* Many stations which opened or closed were not recorded.

## EXPLANATION OF THE MAP OF SIERRA LEONE PROTECTORATE.

The rivers are marked with Roman numerals, beginning at the north. I, Great Skarcies; II, Little Skarcies; III, Sierra Leone; IV, Rokell; V, Ribbi; VI, Bompeh; VII, Cockboro; VIII, Yaltukka; IX, Bargru; X, Sherbro; XI, Jong, or Taia; XII, Bum, or Schwa; XIII, Kittam; XIV, Sulima; XV, Mano.

The mission stations of our Church are marked by a (*) star; other important towns with a circle, or dot. They are numbered with Arabic figures, as follows: 1, Freetown; 11, Waterloo; 2½, Kent; 3½, Port Loko—these are important English Church stations; 2, Rotufunk, Palli, and Bompeh; 3, Makundo; 4, Rokon; 5, Kwallu; 6, Taiama; 7, Mongherri; 8, Tungea—these are under the Woman's Mission Board; 9, Shaingay; 10, Rembee; 11, Mocobo; 12, Otterbein; 13, Jehovah; 14, Tongolo, 15, Ma Sandu; 16, Mandoh; 17, Daymah; 18, Bonthe; 19, Avery; 20, Mano (Mendi); 21, Damballah—these are under the General Mission Board; 22, Gbambiah, under the Radical U. B. Board; 23, Mafwa; 24, Tikonko; 25, Sa; 26, Panguma; 27, Kaure Lahm; 28, Yandahu; 29, Juru; 30, Bandasuma; 31, Koinadugu; 32, Tobabadugu; 33, Falaba.

The routes are marked with broken lines. Note the one from Freetown to Falaba, northeast, into the Sudan; also the route east from Freetown through Rotufunk, Taiami, Mongherri, then northeast through Tungea to Falaba. This is the route inland proposed for the Woman's Board. The route from Avery (19), through Mano (20), Jama, Damballah, Sa, Panguma, to Kaure Lahm is the route inland proposed for the General Board. The railway is now completed from Freetown to Waterloo, and it is proposed to run it on through Rotufunk, Taiama, Mongherri, and Panguma, to the east limit of the Protectorate.

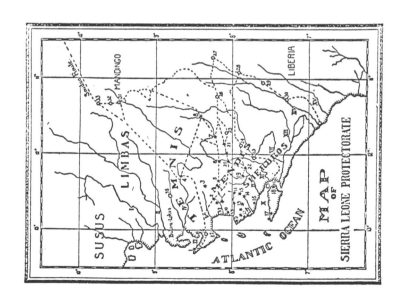

MAP of SIERRA LEONE PROTECTORATE

or not there were any converts. They taught industry and agriculture as well as "book." Three had medical work as well. Schools were opened to gain the confidence and friendship of the people, to attain a permanency to the efforts, and, in the case of boarding schools, to shield the students from many vicious influences.

One of the problems which arises from the school approach is the change in emphasis from evangelism to school improvement and social uplift. Impatience with the slowness of people to turn to Christ often resolves itself into school work which has observable results. The minister in charge of the Bompeh District reported, in 1903, that one of the most gratifying features of the work was the growing interest in education which, if properly encouraged and carried forward, would result in great good to the people.

A missionary lamented in 1938 that

> we have not always given the Church its rightful place in our planning but have gone forward with our school program at the expense of planting, fostering and developing the Church. We seem more anxious to report large numbers on the roll of the school than we are to present large enrollment in our training classes of the Church (1938: 17).

Many teacher-agents are zealous for the growth of the Church, but many more confine their interest to their schools and local church services, tending to let their itinerating among the villages be for the purpose of enrolling more students in their schools rather than preaching the Good News and inviting the people to turn to Christ.

In 1921 the hindrance of the school approach to church growth was recognized, even though nothing was done to rectify it. A report before the annual conference (1921: 11-16) referred to people movements which were happening in other countries but not in Sierra Leone. The reasons given for their absence in Sierra Leone were (1) advanced civilization and (2) the language barrier. The report stated that *most work was done in English*. It began that way in the Colony and continued in the Provinces. All educational and religious work was conducted in a foreign tongue and cast in foreign molds, resulting in a foreign culture. The masses have not been won because the natives have learned from the school system that acceptance of Christianity carries with it the necessity of accepting a foreign culture. Further, the education of their sons and daughters alienates them from their culture.

Learning is of two kinds — direct, and indirect or marginal. People not only listen to what is taught or preached, and interpret what is said according to their preconceptions and prejudices, they also observe and interpret activities and emphases. Thus they often "learn" things far different from what the missionary is advocating. The main thing "learned" from an evangelistic approach which emphasizes western education and civilization is that a person must go to school and be civilized before he can become Christian. Many tribesmen have said they cannot become Christian because they cannot go to school.

Two circuits in the Evangelical United Brethren Church which illustrate the failure of the school approach to win the tribesmen are Jaiama (Kono) and Bonthe. (See the graph on page 157.)

*Jaiama Circuit (Kono)*

At Jaiama the school approach was later coupled with a hospital. To start a school, boys had to be paid to enroll and to live at the school as boarders. Graduates were employed to start schools in the outlying chiefdoms. The purpose of a hospital, besides healing people, was to gain prestige for Christianity. A letter from the Acting Secretary of the Foreign Missionary Society, June 28, 1921, read,

> If our doctors later on perform a few successful surgical operations [on goiters] in Kono they will make a great name for themselves and the mission. This will be a great help as Mohammedan influence is pretty strong there and Mohammedan doctors are pretty influential, but they know nothing about surgery.

In 1965 a team investigated the unfinished missionary task in the twenty-one newly independent nations between the River Senegal and the River Congo. At a consultation convened at Yaounde, Cameroun, in June, 1965, the team reported that the Kono tribe in Sierra Leone has been ignored by the Christians (Taylor 1965: 1-2). It is not true that Christians have ignored the Kono. The Evangelical United Brethren Church (1965) was properly disturbed that its fifty-five years of missionary work had been overlooked.*

However, the report reveals a stark fact: Among the Kono, the school and medical approach has failed to win many people to Christ and to plant strong indigenous churches. The great majority of converts in Kono under the school approach have been students; and the great majority of the converted students have lapsed after completing school.

Two examples illustrate the failure. In 1919 a school was opened at Kayima, a paramount chief town (see the people movement map on page 119). Thirty-one years later, in 1950, an agricultural missionary was stationed there for eleven months. In 1964 the school enrollment was 298, with a teaching staff of nine. None of the teachers itinerated to other villages to preach the Gospel. Church attendance was almost exclusively school children. Very few of the townspeople who had been educated at the school attended church. Very few of the teachers or their wives attended regularly, most only if they were in charge of the service that Sunday. Most of the townspeople who went to church went to the Church of the Lord, Aladura (about two hundred), or God Is Our Light Church (about one hundred). More will be said later of these Churches. The story of Kayima with a "school children" church and non-itinerating teachers is typical.

At the other side of Konoland the townspeople of Gahun are coming to Christ and into the Methodist Church as part of the Methodist people movement which is spreading from the Mende to the Kono. The Evangelical United Brethren school, although present before the people became Methodist, made no attempt to win the people. Obviously it had nothing to do with church growth.**

The team's report at Yaounde overlooked the Christian activity in Konoland. What small growth is occurring in the Jaiama Circuit of the Evangelical United Brethren Church is

* Letter from the field representative of the Evangelical United Brethren Mission, December 2, 1965.
** Interviews with the Methodist Circuit Superintendent, the Evangelical United Brethren District Minister, and an Evangelical United Brethren evangelist.

caused not through the opening and operating of schools, but through the efforts of a few church-minded teachers and evangelists (full-time, paid pastor-itinerators). The greatest ingathering of Kono people (including the people of Gahun) into the Kingdom of God, however, is within the people movement in the Methodist Manowa-Penguia Circuit, with headquarters at Sandaru.

*Bonthe Circuit*

The growth of the Bonthe Circuit was exclusively in the Bonthe Church until 1951, although there were many outstation school churches. Decline in the church followed the exodus of citizens when many of the town businesses closed. After 1954 growth occurred in some of the outstations through the itineration of some of the teacher-agents. In a few cases Christianity broke through the school barrier to reach some of the townsmen and surrounding villagers, e.g., Yoni-Sherbro and Commendi-Jono). Since that year, most growth, however, has been due to tiny movements in each of the twenty-one outstations. Lack of reliable water transportation prevents the District Minister from giving the kind of supervision which would lead to stronger churches and greater outreach.

The school approach probably was necessary at the beginning of the mission to gain a foothold in a hostile land. A foothold was gained by 1875, but a new strategy was not sought. The first attempt to open a station without a mission school was in 1949 at Mongere, where the mission school had failed earlier and a government school had opened.

Sierra Leone needs schools. The needs of the people, the prestige of having many schools, and competition with the Roman Catholics are forcing Protestants to continue their school emphasis. This emphasis, however, must not usurp the primary aim of the Church: winning the people to Christ and forming them into growing indigenous churches. Churches must recognize that schools do not evangelize adults, but educate children and evangelize a few of them.

ORGANIZATIONAL STRUCTURE AND THE MINISTRY

In 1877, twenty years after the founding of the mission

station at Shenge, a theological school was erected for the purpose of training "indigenous leadership," meaning western-ized-civilized leadership. Some students who completed school were employed as teacher-agents (or teacher-preachers) to open other schools and hold services.

Those who did well were trained in short courses to be ministers while they remained in charge of the churches as-signed to them. The course of study adopted was the same reading course, with no adaptations, which the ministers in the United States followed. In 1907 a four-week Theological Institute was organized to help candidates for the ministry master the books of the reading course. In more recent years some candidates for the ministry received additional theological education at Fourah Bay College in Freetown (now the Uni-versity College of Sierra Leone). This is no longer practiced, however.

In 1912 a system of direct supervision was started in which the smaller stations were put under the supervision of older ministers and missionaries. Up to this time the missionary-conference superintendent, who was also principal of Albert Academy, a secondary school in Freetown, had assumed the burden of supervision. Four years later the quarterly confer-ence system was begun. The territory was divided into nine areas, each with a quarterly conference. The immediate pur-pose of the quarterly conference was for the paid workers and lay officials within its area to meet for two or three days at the close of each quarter "for Bible study and prayer; to make a report of the work done during the quarter under review; to submit records and accounts for inspection; to counsel on everyday problems; to plan for the future; to grant lay and quarterly conference preachers' licenses" (Annual Re-port of the West African Mission to the Home Board 1916).

The long-range purpose of this system was the complete evangelization of all the villages and towns within each assigned quarterly conference area — 5000 villages, or approximately 150 towns for every station then occupied. The report said:

> The workers in quarterly conference areas are being asked to undertake definite extension work by supporting young men as evangelists and teachers in towns not yet occupied. ... We believe that such a step is vital to the growth of

the native church. They must be definitely and actively enlisted in giving the gospel to others to make it more vitally their own.

A task of this magnitude, the evangelization of the masses, with a primitive environment in Pagan Africa, who live in 5,000 towns, cannot be done in a day or by attempting it in a small way. There is no telling what the resources of the native church will prove to be in men and money if it gives itself over to the task. And while we will look to the native church and schools to produce the men who will actually go into the towns, it would hardly be able to give money in large enough sums to support the work should it develop as we might hope, yet she may.

The home church must provide in a large measure for the supervision of this work.

The work of an evangelistic missionary would be to have direct supervision of a group of churches and all extension work done within a prescribed area. He would not only be given oversight of all the stations of the quarterly conference, but he would develop the work in the hundreds of towns to be evangelized. Our churches never had the kind of supervision they should have. But it would be utterly impossible and useless to attempt what we propose above in fully evangelizing the territory we now occupy unless we attempt it under the most rigid system of supervision.

The type of work we now propose has not been done in Sierra Leone. It more nearly approaches the methods used in the successful missions in Nigeria, the Congo and the Cameroons.

Every district prescribed as a quarterly conference area with perhaps some modification, should be supervised by an ordained man with the best possible training, and most of these for years to come should be missionaries.

The organization was set up, but because of World War I, then in progress, extra missionaries with which to implement the program were not forthcoming. Evangelism was the great desire, but schools and paid workers were the means chosen to do the evangelizing. More will be said later regarding the paid workers. To this date, with a few exceptions, the villages, although evangelized, have not been discipled with planted churches. Even within most of the stations "many native people look upon the church as a foreign institution and the services are attended by the mission group but the people of the community do not" (*Journal* 1937: 23).

Through the years the number of ordained ministers increased until they outnumbered the ordained missionaries. Eventually an African was elected as Conference Superintendent (the executive officer of the Evangelical United Brethren Church). Later there were two. The Conference was divided into two "areas" with a Conference Superintendent in charge of each. Both were pastors of large churches, the largest two of the Conference, and so were only part-time superintendents. Now there is one full-time Conference Superintendent. He supervises the main churches served by ministers, most of whom are District Ministers.

The District Minister* is responsible for management of the schools in his district, for payment of salaries to teachers, teacher-agents, and evangelists, and for collection of money the Conference assesses each church for conference expenses. In carrying out these duties, he acts as paymaster for Church and government. He is expected to visit all the stations in his district to advise the evangelists or teacher-agents in charge, to baptize and receive persons into membership, and to give communion. These involve spiritual supervision — the kind of supervision which ought to yield both stronger churches and wider church planting. Many District Ministers do not do this kind of supervising. Thus supervision is poor, and teacher-agents and evangelists are left to work on their own. Many of the districts are large in both area and number of outstations, and after the minister has cared for the duties of his own church and school, he finds little time to do more than

* The District Ministers of the Evangelical United Brethren Church do not have the authority of the Circuit Superintendents of the Methodist Church. The Methodist Annual Synod assigns ministers and catechists to a circuit and appoints one of the ministers as Circuit Superintendent. He has the authority to station the ministers and catechists within the circuit, and can make changes within the circuit if he considers it necessary.

The Evangelical United Brethren Annual Conference, on the other hand, stations all ministers, evangelists, and teacher-agents and appoints those ministers who will serve as District Ministers. A District Minister wanting changes in stationing within his district must ask the Conference Superintendent to do it.

handle the monthly financial matters of the other stations within his district. Ecclesiastical machinery takes all his time. Little is left for church multiplication.

In 1952 the last two persons taking the reading course in the annual four-week Theological Institute were ordained, and the work of the Institute ceased. It was not until 1963 that it was resumed. Meanwhile, the ranks of the active ministry were being depleted because ministers were being elected to government positions and there were no new recruits. Students from Albert Academy, formerly the main source of the ministry, were no longer being motivated to become ministers. Some of the reasons were: (1) vigorous recruiting and follow-up were lacking, (2) ministers received less salary than most educated men desired, and (3) the attitudes and example of some ministers did not encourage young men to consider the ministry or to persevere in training for the ministry if they did consider it.

Part of the answer to the problem was found in the Bible Training Institute at Bo. Through the influence of one missionary, and against the desires of both the mission board in Dayton, Ohio, and the Conference, the Institute began in 1952. In 1949, Conference made an attempt to cooperate in a joint Bible School with the American Wesleyan Methodists at Gbendembu. Ordination was one of the reasons it did not succeed. The American Wesleyan Methodists would ordain their students after graduation but the Evangelical United Brethren would not. So the Bible Training Institute was founded to train as evangelists those who did not have sufficient academic background to be ordained.

Despite initial disapproval, the value of the Institute was quickly realized. (1) It provided evangelists for existing out-stations where teachers were tied up in the school work and were not itinerating, and (2) it enabled many new stations to be opened. The outstanding fruit of the Bible Training Institute has been the people movements in the Mongere and Mondema areas (see the people movement map on page 119) under the leadership of four of the first graduates. The growth in many of the circuits since 1955 has been due to the itinerating of these evangelists who could spend full time preaching the Gospel and persuading men to become disciples of Christ. Two reasons for success are: (1) evangelists are not as culturally removed from the people as are the ministers; and (2) they know they are expected to itinerate and go to localities where the people are. Many of the evangelists, however, do no better in reaching beyond the gathered static Christian community of the local church than do many of the ministers and teacher-agents.

The Evangelical United Brethren Church in America, with ministers and people on the same social level, has a one-level ministry. This pattern was transported by missionaries to Sierra Leone where ministers were elevated to a different level from the people. As long as the outstations remained few, the pattern seemed to work, because missionaries, and later the national ministers, could serve both their own churches and the outstations. However, the outstations could not become "full" churches because their pastors were not ordained and the members were dependent for the sacraments upon the occasional visits of an outsider who was culturally separated from them and did not understand them.

As the number of outstations increased and the number of active ministers decreased, the remote outstation churches were neglected, especially with respect to receiving communion. The problem was greatly increased when small village churches around the outstations emerged, because it became physically impossible for many ministers to serve communion to all the congregations in their districts. The American ministerial system is not equipped to meet this kind of situation. The result is central local churches with the sacraments and many outstation churches without the sacraments.

Another contrast between central and outstation churches is the kind of people being served. Educated tribesmen predominate in the central churches. Nonliterates are in the majority in many of the outstation churches, and particularly in the small village churches (if there are any) around the outstations. Sierra Leone has, therefore, a two-level society — one educated and western, and the other nonwestern, with people who believe in witches, malevolent spirits, ancestral spirits, magic, and curses. The Evangelical United Brethren Church is training ministers for the western level, which it must continue doing at a greater rate. It is not training ministers for the nonwestern level, which is where the masses are. At present many of the evangelists and teacher-agents serve the nonwestern level.

The situation requires a two-level ordained ministry. Present evangelists and teacher-agents who have proved themselves mature and able pastors and church planters ought to receive short courses to help them minister at the level where they are and then be ordained to minister with full authority to that level. Those intellectually able to pursue deeper western education should be given further short courses to help them minister at the central church level. The majority of recruits for the latter should, however, be from secondary school graduates.

In both levels much more needs to be taught on the popular level. Dr. A. R. Tippett writes,

> The value of academic training lies not in mental exercise or in mere interest, but in its ultimate validity and applicability in a missionary ministry. . . .
>
> Weaknesses in curricula are often reflections of weaknesses in basic texts for study. When one considers the wealth of material at the metaphysical level (all very much needed), one is appalled at the dearth of it at the popular level; yet its problems are just as great and just as urgent (1960: 412-413).

Beginning in 1966 the Bible Training Institute in Bo has been trying to provide education through a two-year Lay Preachers' Course for untrained evangelists and teacher-agents — persons who serve at the "popular level." The main entrance requirements are that the person be an active church leader and be literate in English. An Evangelical United Brethren student satisfactorily completing the course may (if approved by annual conference) become a "local lay preacher" with authority to administer the sacraments in his station or parish. But he would not be an ordained minister with privileges of voting in the annual conference session.

## MONEY

The system of workers being sent by, paid by, and responsible to the Conference is well established and is ingrained into the thinking of Conference leaders, of paid workers, and of church members. Talk of using volunteers as church leaders recurs, but the thought of training them to be official conference pastors of their churches never arises.

Often Christians have come together in towns on account of government work or business and have automatically looked to the Conference ("Mission" as they still call it) for evangelists. What they really are asking for are chaplains to conduct services for them. One of their own number could easily perform the duties, but the people have been taught dependence.

Many missiologists have pointed out the dangers in paying agents to itinerate and preach. Roland Allen, late Anglican missionary to China under the Society for the Propagation of the Gospel (SPG), is one of the best known. In his book, *The Spontaneous Expansion of the Church,* one of the dangers he presents is, if an agent is paid to preach

> both speaker and hearer are affected by that fact. The speaker knows, and knows that the other knows, that he is employed by a mission to speak. He is not delivering his own message because he cannot help it. He is not speaking of Christ because Christ alone impels him. Do men not ask our paid agents: "How much are you paid for the work?" And must they not answer? And does not the answer destroy the [effectiveness of the message] (1960: 11)?

Many evangelists are chronic grumblers. This also influences the effectiveness of their message. The greatest complaint is money. They often feel they are paid too little and that they are sent out as money collectors rather than as "good news bringers" and church pastors. The concern of Conference seems to them solely to be whether each church has paid its assessment. If a church has not, the evangelist (who is paid by Conference) is called to account. The evangelist usually forestalls such accounting by paying the assessment from his salary. If the payments are up to date and the church is running smoothly financially, whether the church is growing or dying, the evangelist hears not a word from Conference. The District Minister, who is the paymaster, usually sees to it that the assessments are paid, for if they are not he also will be called to account. In some cases agreements are made whereby the assessments are deducted from the evangelists' salaries.

Emphasis on money disturbs relationships between evangelists and their superiors. More important, it distracts attention from church growth to finances. This is true both on the conference level and in the local church. Reyburn put it clearly:

> The orientation of Christian missions is definitely cast in a financial mold which it brings from its home churches and ecclesiastical heritage, in which self-propagation means often that the local church needs to pay the catechist or pastor and keep books. This is to the missionary a mere step which the indigenes must learn if they are to be a self-supporting church. Actually many native churches would be self-supporting if missionaries had not made such an issue of it and caused it to become a front line aspect of the missionizing movement. European backgrounds with money-conscious values and organizations have in effect often impressed native groups that upon the financial handling of the church depends everything else. Consequently the conceptualization of the church has often been in the natives' mind a kind of primitive bank in which everyone is a member of the board. There is probably nothing in the native churches of ... today which merits one tenth of the time taken up in budgets and money matters (1959 6:16).

In all the local church council meetings I attended in Sierra Leone, nine-tenths to ten-tenths of the time was spent discussing money. The indigenous approach which trains voluntary leaders would go a long way toward solving the money problem.

Merle Davis in his book *How the Church Grows in Brazil* discusses the difficulty village churches face in becoming self-supporting when they are served by a highly educated pastor.

> A yet greater difficulty is the inability for the rural congregation to pay the salary required by a pastor who has taken the long course of education for the ministry. The rural community in Brazil is living close to the subsistence level. The appearance in their midst of a family of non-producers whom they must support is a disaster. It upsets the economic balance of the community and introduces a type of life entirely outside of their experience. The Evangelical Church, as brought to Brazil, is a middle class institution and requires the economic margin for support that is provided by the incomes of a middle class. The ministry, too, is a middle class profession and for support requires a

middle class economy. The presence of a large middle class in Brazilian cities has made possible the financial independence of the urban church. However, by and large, there is no middle class in the Brazilian hinterland (1943: 68-69).

Then, should the workers receive no pay, or at least receive none from conference funds? No single answer can be given because circumstances vary. The Nevius Method of planting and developing indigenous churches (1958) prohibits the payment of native preachers or the building of local churches from mission funds (except for certain limited cases) and requires (1) propagation of the Gospel by voluntary agents who remain in their occupations, and (2) self-support from emerging churches from the beginning. The system was implemented in Korea beginning in the 1890s. In some situations it worked to produce great growth; in others it did not. When the people were ripe for harvest into the Kingdom of God it worked. Roy Shearer, missionary to Korea, reports:

> Without a doubt, the Nevius policy was the best policy for growth in the north-west of Korea. It allowed the spreading Church to be free of the shackles of foreign money. When a new church was erected, New York did not have to be consulted for building funds.
>
> The Methodists [American] working in the same area were reported by William Hunt in 1909 to be using American funds for building and for paying helpers. But he reports that this use of American church funds caused trouble of all kinds. The Methodist Church could grow only as fast as the money for buildings and pastors' salaries could be provided by the missionaries, while the adjacent Presbyterian Church, free of foreign control and funds but with plenty of working assistance from dedicated foreigners, grew rapidly. To put it simply: the Nevius Method worked in the north-west (1965 54: 466-467).

Where the people were not ripe the method did not work to produce growth. In poverty-ridden, unripe areas it actually retarded growth. Shearer concludes that "the Nevius missionary plan worked well where the Korean people were responsive, but that its rigid use in less responsive areas of Korea actually retarded church growth."

The Nevius Method has not been tried in Sierra Leone. But if responsive areas are to grow spontaneously, it must be tried. Some situations need paid pastors, others do not. City churches require full-time paid pastors and can pay them without conference subsidy. Static outstation churches could survive just as well through voluntary members who are given extra training for the task with occasional supervision. However, systematic itinerating with the goal of planting churches in the surrounding villages would probably require conference-paid evangelists. Even so, the planted churches must be taught self-leadership. Voluntary leaders must be trained to pastor their churches and to itinerate. The evangelist would thus be a supervisor and a pastor to the overall parish. Needless to say, his pastorate would be incomplete without authority to give the sacraments.

## DEVOLUTION

The transfer of authority from mission to Church in Sierra Leone points to a truth seldom recognized in missionary circles. *Devolution which occurs as part of the school approach creates a dictatorial type of national leadership which prevents the maximum expansion of the Church.* The Evangelical United Brethren Church exhibits one typical path which many Missions travel. The chart on opposite page diagrams the process.

Having outlined the process of devolution in the Evangelical United Brethren Church, we now turn to the lessons it has for us. Mission boards and societies have often considered stage two necessary in the devolution of a mission, and place it in their program of progress. On the contrary, it is detrimental to the growth of the Church. Stage one should pass into stage three directly. The missionary should transfer authority voluntarily as soon as there is a group of believers. He should not abnegate responsibility to the congregation, but should give it guidance in choosing and training unpaid leaders. (Henceforth, these will be called Class I leaders.) This is devolution beginning at the grass roots — at the lowest level.

As soon as several congregations have been organized, the unpaid leaders who have proved themselves by voluntarily

# DEVOLUTION IN THE
# EVANGELICAL UNITED BRETHREN CHURCH

### Stage One
### Mission Domination

The Mission dominated institutions, churches, and leadership, and made little effort to raise leaders at grass roots level and give them local authority.

Leaders were trained from their youth in the western way to resemble the American pattern of leadership and were sent out to start schools and congregations.

The teacher became the sole leader in the little congregation which emerged with little or no encouragement of local leadership.

Eventually some ministers were trained well enough in the American way to be entrusted with limited supervisory positions.

### Transition
Domination yielded resentment creating tension.

### Stage Two
### Separation of Mission and Church with Conference
### (African) Domination

Conference dominated in church affairs after the pattern of the Mission in stage one.

The authority of evangelistic missionaries was so restricted that they were rendered almost ineffective in helping churches grow.

At first the Mission still dominated in social service. By 1965 nationals were in full control except in community development.

A Joint Council was created to permit discussion on general program between nationals and missionaries.

| Conference set of committees | Joint Council set of committees | Mission Council set of committees |
|---|---|---|

### Transition
Time heals wounds and suspicions.

### Stage Three
### Reintegration of Mission and Church
### (Implemented in 1966)

Nationals are the top leaders, but missionaries participate in conference committees and boards.

Evangelistic missionaries are assigned as circuit ministers with supervisory authority over evangelists within their circuits.

bringing the Gospel to other villages and by successfully leading the villagers to Christ (these will be called Class II leaders), should be trained further, and those among them who
have been called of God to the ministry should be given authority, i.e., ordained, to supervise groups of villages, to be
their pastors, and to receive some material assistance (remuneration) so they can spend full time at their task. (These slightly
trained and paid leaders will be called Class III leaders.)

Some of these leaders who are educated in English and
have proved themselves through church service should receive
further training to equip them to be district ministers and
ministers of city churches where educated people are. (These
well-paid and trained men will be called Class IV leaders.)
From among these will be elected conference superintendents.

Thus devolution should occur at each step in the growth
of the Church. At each level the indigenous leaders should
assume the dominant roles in committees and conferences with
the missionaries in the background ready to help. At the lower
levels, if a serious blunder should occur or if a church stag-
nates, the missionary should assume the dominant role and
correct the problem, if possible. By the time a conference
superintendent is elected from among the Class IV leaders
devolution will be complete.

The school approach militates against the above program
of devolution and causes the necessity of stage two. This program (or indigenous approach) assumes the conversion of
many nonliterates, works among them, and trains them by
establishing schools — schools which not only teach children
but also teach adults. Adults who are accustomed to leading
can be taught to use their leadership ability in the church.

But the school approach has conversions chiefly from
among the school children. These children are taught dependence from their youth up, so usually are not equipped to become strong leaders on their own. They constantly need advice.
Even as the missionary does everything for them, so they do
everything for the churches they serve. Marginally the tribespeople learn that not only must a person go to school to become
a Christian, but he must also have been to school if he is to
be a leader in the church.

Domination spawns dependency and dependency requires domination. A vicious circle develops. Eventually the missionary assumes the perpetual necessity of domination. When the dependent national rebels, the missionary is surprised, and tension mounts and precipitates stage two. One side effect of marginal learning within this pattern which sinks into the dominated dependent national is the pattern itself. "Raise up a child in the way he should go, and he will not depart from it." "As a parent is, so is the child." "The sins of the fathers will be visited upon the children to the third and fourth generation." Class IV leaders (educated nationals in charge of churches or circuits) tend to dominate Class III leaders (paid itinerators, evangelists, and catechists), who in turn tend to dominate local churches and whatever Class I or II leaders there may be. Devolution is not only the problem of the Mission; it is also the problem of the emergent Church.

To break the circle of domination and dependency, the school approach to evangelism and church planting must be replaced by the indigenous approach and a conscious effort on the part of all leaders to encourage independence in the lower levels of leadership. The Church will be able to grow at its maximum rate when domination from the top down is replaced by leadership from the bottom up.

Devolution from the Church Missionary Society to the Sierra Leone Church failed to result in missionary outreach. Devolution need not end evangelization of the tribes, but the danger is always there. S. A. J. Pratt's judgment of the Churches working in the hinterland is,

> These did magnificent evangelistic work in the past, until· later they followed the pattern of the Colony Churches and concentrated their ministry mainly on converted Christians (1956: 8).

Unfortunately, this is true of most of the Evangelical United Brethren churches. It was true in stage one when missionaries dominated, and remains true today in stage three. But it need not remain true.

The new organizational structure in stage three has a Board of Evangelism and Mission in which ideally evangelistically minded ministers, laymen, and missionaries work together. If this board were to meet regularly to make bold plans for church growth, and if the executive committee of Conference (Conference Council of Administration) were to give the board full support by carrying out the plans, then devolution would yield church growth and strength.

A primary goal of missions and devolution is to produce a missionary Church with missionary congregations. A comprehensive program must be planned to achieve this.

However, the first two years of stage three (1966-68) has shown that the Conference does not know how to formulate such a program. In the past, the Conference made goals but left it to individual ministers to find means of achieving them. No comprehensive program of goals and means, bringing together all phases of church work into a harmonious whole with adequate supervision, has ever been achieved. Consequently, various programs often proceed at their own momentum, sometimes at cross-purposes.

## CHURCH GROWTH

The Evangelical United Brethren have enjoyed greater growth among the tribes in Sierra Leone than have any of the other Churches (see graph page 74), yet most of its churches are static. The graph on page 157 compares five of the thirteen circuits of the Church, and the summary below the graph illustrates the variety in kinds of church growth.

### Taiama Parish*

The greatest church growth in Sierra Leone is taking place in people movements (see the map on page 119). Of these, Taiama Parish is the most successful. Here about seven thousand souls are Christian, although only twenty-one hundred are full baptized members. The religious distribution map on page 46 shows this parish as the only area marked "50% to 75% Christian." It is called a parish because the many village

* Information regarding Taiama Parish and its program is from an interview with the Rev. B. A. Carew, a Sierra Leonean, who was pastor at the time of the interview.

EVANGELICAL UNITED BRETHREN CHURCH

Membership Comparison of Five Circuits

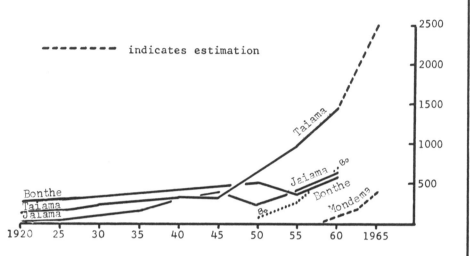

Summary of Kinds of Growth

• The Taiama Circuit line represents people movement growth
  around Taiama and no growth in the outstations.

• The Bonthe Circuit line represents Bonthe Church growth up
  until 1951 and outstation growth after 1954.

• The Jaiama Circuit line represents diamond miner growth,
  some outstation growth, and many static outstations.

• The Bo Circuit line represents mostly town transfer growth
  in Bo, static outstations, and people movement growth
  around Mongere.

• The Mondema Circuit line represents people movement growth.

congregations surounding Taiama are all considered to be part of Taiama Church, and the pastor at the church is also the pastor of all the 110 village congregations (in 1964) as well as District Minister and Conference Superintendent. Although missionaries have been resident at Taiama since before the Hut Tax War, and although a dispensary and maternity clinic has been operating there for as many years, the main growth did not occur until after the present pastor was stationed there in 1937. He attributes the success to (1) much *prayer,* (2) regular systematic *itineration* to proclaim the Gospel to all the villages of the chiefdom every month, (3) *organization* of the converts into village congregations and the village congregations into groups or sections, and (4) *training* of village congregation leadership.

The villages vary in size from twenty to two hundred adult population. The 110 villages of the parish are organized into fourteen sections, one village in each section being designated the section village. Most of the villages have worship leaders (Class I leaders). The section leaders (Class II leaders) are responsible for visiting all the churches within their sections once a month. All worship and section leaders are voluntary. When the parish was smaller and the pastor had no other responsibility, he had regular contact with all the villages. Now he supervises through the section congregations. All Christians of a section must meet him at the section center. He is assisted by a paid church visitor who conducts funerals and visits all the villages monthly for exhortation.

The parish has two business committees. (1) The parish board, with representatives from the village congregations, makes plans for the parish. These plans are submitted to (2) the executive committee of Taiama Church, which comprises elected educated townspeople. The executive committee has final authority over the village congregations.

All parish activities revolve around Taiama. Members in nearby villages are expected to come to Taiama for worship every Sunday morning and to have their own services on Sunday and Thursday evenings. Members farther than eight miles (the farthest is fifteen miles) are to come as often as possible, but are required to come four times a year and on special occasions. After each Sunday morning worship service at the parsonage, the pastor provides a fellowship meal and a weekly supply of anti-malaria pills for those who come from the surrounding villages. Communion is given once a quarter and only at Taiama.

Annually a spiritual life crusade is held to enroll those who desire and are eligible for baptism. They are given four months training by their section leaders, after which they all come to Taiama for baptism in the river. Those too infirm to be immersed are baptized in a separate ceremony at the church. Reception into membership, in a special service, follows soon after baptism.

Because Taiama is the center, with many programs to unite the Christians, its members have a strong sense of Christian solidarity. They are proud to belong to Taiama Church. Some Christians come from afar, bypassing outstation churches to come to Taiama.

The parish structure is patterned after the chiefdom structure. Chiefdoms are divided into sections with section chiefs, and then into towns and villages, each with its chief. The practice of having all important events at Taiama is patterned after the Wundi secret society. All meetings of that society are held at the paramount chief town, Taiama, so the people are accustomed to coming there for meetings and rituals.

Each secret society in Sierra Leone has a ladder of membership status. Before each rung or level may be attained, certain requirements must be met. To a certain degree, this pattern has been adopted by the church. The church has two levels of affiliation. (1) Conversion, evidenced by attending church regularly, giving offerings, forsaking charms and pagan or Muslim sacrifices, and giving up drunkenness, brings people into the first level. Their names are written down and they are considered part of the church. At this level some become strong Christians, but many remain marginal, attending church very seldom; or nominal, never attending. The latter have their names removed from the records; however, unless they actually identify themselves as Muslims or pagans,* they are

* My research into the Taiama Parish revealed some Christians who had become Muslim, but none who had reverted to paganism.

considered by the people of the villages still to be Christians. (2) Giving up polygamy permits the Christian (after being trained for baptism) to enter the second level. Christians on this level are full members and may receive communion and hold office in the church.

Churches multiplied because the pastor preached the Good News of Jesus Christ in the villages and urged the people to turn to Christ and form worshipping groups. Although the emphasis was on individual conversion, the movement to Christ followed the web of family relationships. The village congregations I visited in the parish said they became Christian because of an itinerant preacher, either a paid worker, a voluntary itinerator, or (in one case) a missionary. None said they turned to Christ because they were urged to by relatives. However, within any one village most of those who turned to Christ did so within a short period of one or two years. So, although they attributed their conversion to an itinerator, those within a village or family who became Christian first must have had much influence on the others. McGavran calls this kind of people movement to Christ a web movement, because conversion follows the web of family relationships. In nine of the eleven villages I visited, the majority of the villagers (in two villages all but three persons) considered themselves Christians, although less than half of these had been baptized. At Taiama the greatest hindrances to baptism are polygamy and irregular church attendance.

An annual two-to-four-week church life institute at Taiama provides leadership training for the village congregations. Vernacular literacy, Bible, farming, and health make up the usual curriculum. Recently, English literacy has been added. All the village congregations I visited were led in local worship services by vernacular leaders who had been trained at the church life institute. Persons who attend are responsible for their own travel, food, lodging, and study materials. Instructors are missionaries, school-teachers, government literacy teachers, and others who require no financial remuneration from Taiama Church. Thus the institute is self-supporting.

Currently, growth of Taiama Parish is occurring on the outskirts of the parish. All except one of the villages I visited had been Christian before 1956. The problem now facing the parish is its size. William Read, in his book *New Patterns of Church Growth in Brazil,* examines the "mother church plan," which is responsible for tens of thousands of converts in Brazil. This plan is comparable to the parish plan of the Taiama Church. Commenting on the plan Read observes,

> There comes, however, a saturation point in the growth of these Mother Churches. If they do not decentralize, they fossilize and lose their effectiveness as agents for evangelism and dynamic church growth (1965: 170).

The parish is dependent upon Taiama. It has no authority to make and carry out its own plans. The townspeople in the executive committee have the final say. Leadership training for village congregation life is provided, but not for evangelistic outreach. Nor are sections of the parish being brought to selfhood. This dependence is due to the pattern of relying solely on educated persons for this kind of leadership. Only evangelists and teacher-agents are considered able to handle such responsibility. Therefore, only as such are available can sections become separate parishes.

For example, an evangelist was stationed in one section to make it a separate parish, and the members of the section rejoiced. It revitalized the church. However, only one of the village congregations of the section chose to become part of the new parish, all the others choosing to remain with Taiama. The new parish (as the other outstations of the circuit) does not have the sacraments as an integral part of its life; and it is still under the authority of Taiama. All the church gained was that members do not have to walk the four miles to Taiama. This is offset somewhat by their having to pay part of the salary of their lay pastor (evangelist). Since members of the other village congregations have to walk anyway, they choose to walk to Taiama, if at all.

It is unlikely that clusters (sections) of congregations close to Taiama could, or should, become separate parishes, but the outlying ones should. Only thus can they exert the evangelistic effort necessary to multiply village congregations. New parishes, to be more effective in their outreach, ought to have authority to give the sacraments; then converts will know that they are entering a complete church.

The people within Taiama Circuit (which comprises Tai-ama Parish plus thirteen outstations in the area beyond) are homogeneous. They are similar in language, cultural back-ground, and amount of Islamic influence. Yet good growth is occurring only in Taiama Parish. The graph on the follow-ing page compares two local churches of the circuit — Taiama and Mano. Taiama has enjoyed the residence of missionaries since before the Hut Tax War. Mano, twelve miles away (see map on page 119), began shortly after the war, when the railroad was being built. The growth within these two towns was nearly the same. In a few years Mano had a few more members than Taiama (1921, 1924-1926). In about 1944, Taiama began to plant village congregations. Mano did not, and all but died. Meanwhile, Christianity began to multiply in the villages around Taiama. The other outstations of Taiama Circuit fared as did Mano, with pitifully little growth — an average of six members per outstation in 1960. (See map on page 119. Squares around Taiama Parish indicate outstations of the circuit.)

Reasons for the static outstations are: (1) Workers did not itinerate to preach Jesus Christ and plant village congre-gations. They were tied to their schools and to the tiny churches. (2) They were not trained to plant churches. (3) They were not trained to prepare and send adult converts out to evangelize and win converts. (4) They had no authority to give the sacraments, and thus the sacraments could not be-come an integral part of the growing church. In contrast, the pastor at Taiama was ordained, so he had authority to give the sacraments. He refused to be tied to the school, and itin-erated to plant village congregations. He itinerated so far that Taiama Parish now includes villages around several of the circuit outstations.

To encourage greater growth, evangelists in the circuit who have proved themselves capable pastors and itinerant soul winners ought to be given further training in how to approach a village as a unit to be won for Christ, and in how to establish evangelistically minded village congregations. They should then be ordained to the first level of the ministry to empower them to give the sacraments so that the sacraments

EVANGELICAL UNITED BRETHREN CHURCH

Comparison of Taiama Church and Mano Church

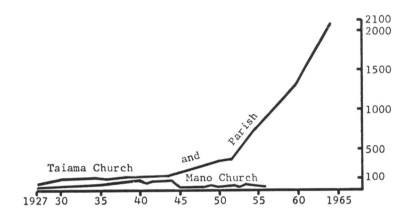

Growth at Taiama grew to include 110 villages. Growth at Mano was confined to Mano town. This graph shows that the way to win Sierra Leone for Christ is to win villagers and plant churches in every town and village throughout the land.

can become an integral part of their ministry and of the planted churches. Further, villages of Taiama Parish near an outstation ought to be transferred to the outstation to make it a parish. Evangelists thus trained and empowered should yield stronger churches and much greater church growth.

## Mongere Parish

Mongere Parish also has been growing sporadically in people movement fashion (see the map on page 119). From 1925 to 1935 over one hundred were enrolled as catechumens, but none was baptized. The evangelist who began the parish plan there, in 1956, followed the Taiama pattern of prayer, itineration, and organization. He adopted the plan of grouping the village congregations into sections, with village and section leaders. He was handicapped, however, by not being empowered to give the sacraments, so that they could become an integral part of the parish. Occasional visits of missionaries (once or twice a year) provided the sacraments. Further, the pattern of always going to the paramount chief town at Mongere was not as strong as at Taiama, so the village members come only for important meetings. Moreover, he did not begin a church life institute to train worship leaders for the village congregations and sections. Instead, he visited some of the leaders in their villages to prepare them for the week's Sunday worship service. Also, for a while he held a weekly class at Mongere for leaders of villages near Mongere.

After seven years of pastoring and discipling, he had a parish of fifty village congregations within a radius of fifteen miles, and an estimated one thousand Christians (less than one-tenth of the adult population of the chiefdom). He was on self-support and the people of the parish had built a chapel at Mongere. All growing village churches have problems. This was true of both Taiama and Mongere. Yet, every indication that the people were ready to turn to Christ was present. All that remained to be done was to gather in the harvest and train village leadership. God had given the Evangelical United Brethren a golden opportunity to thoroughly disciple another chiefdom plus adjacent chiefdoms. Reinforcements were clearly called for.

Then a minister in a growing city church died. Since the evangelist, by then in training for ordination, was the only one both able to fill the vacancy and not serving a circuit headquarters church, he was selected to fill the vacancy. An elderly evangelist who did not believe in itinerating was sent to Mongere. Growth abruptly stopped; attendance fell, and offerings all but ceased. After a few months the evangelist resigned from Mongere (the people were not paying his salary).* One wonders how many God-given opportunities for the growth of His Church are neglected.

Several months later an energetic evangelist who believed in itinerating was sent. Discipling has resumed; but thorough discipling requires reinforcements. The sacraments must become an integral part of the program. The evangelist needs to be ordained to the first level of the ministry. Evangelists presently serving "unripe" fields should be brought to help temporarily in establishing strong village congregations. Perhaps a missionary should be stationed at Mongere as a circuit minister to help supervise the evangelists and strengthen the leadership so that the parish, or parishes, will be well grounded. Clearly the situation calls for bold plans. One function of the newly formed Conference Board of Mission and Evangelism should be to examine statistical records, to identify responsive areas, and to make the necessary bold plans for maximum church growth.

### Mondema Circuit

Mondema Circuit, adjacent to Mongere Parish, is the other Evangelical United Brethren area experiencing people movements. They also were begun in the same manner as at Mongere and Taiama. The area comprises several parishes, each with a center church. From 1964 to 1968 (with one year off for furlough) a missionary was stationed at Mondema** to help train evangelists and other leaders that the churches may be strong with evangelistic outreach. The map on page

* From an interview with S. K. Senesie and with seven congregations of the parish.
** This writer was the missionary stationed at Mondema.

119 indicates that the people movement in one of the parishes is spreading north among the Kono. At present the members of the parishes are not involved in evangelistic efforts. They are allowing the evangelists (Class III leaders) to do all of the evangelistic itineration. More needs to be done to enlist and train voluntary leaders, both to conduct services in local congregations (Class I leaders) and to itinerate as parish-section leaders and as missionaries to villages where there are no Christians (Class II leaders).

The circuit made use of the Methodist (Mende-vernacular) Bible School and Women's Training Centre near Segbwema before the Bible school closed. The Evangelical United Brethren, relying solely on English, have no vernacular training institutions. To train Class II leaders more adequately and to train some to become Class III leaders, the Conference should actively cooperate with the Methodists.

These three areas (Taiama, Mongere, and Mondema), in contrast to the school approach, suggest that itineration to plant village congregations, plus follow-up to strengthen the congregations, win tribespeople to Christ. However, people movements do not expand indefinitely on their own. The history of missions relates numerous stories of people movements which have been allowed to stop prematurely without winning whole tribes to Christ.

Joseph Wold (1968) tells of such an arrested people movement among the Kru in Liberia under the Methodist (American) Mission. Many Kru turned to Christ, and village congregations were planted in a large section of the tribe. Instead of following up the people movement to win the whole tribe for Christ, the missionaries were withdrawn before a self-propagating Kru Church was established. The people movement stopped.

The people movements around Taiama, Mongere, and Mondema could, if handled according to church growth principles, expand indefinitely until the Mende, and adjacent tribes, are thoroughly discipled with strong Christian congregations in all the villages of all the chiefdoms. Impossible? Not at all! The conclusion of this book suggests how the Mende tribe, for example, can be won for Christ.

## BENEVOLENCES

The discussion of church growth indicated that large segments of the tribespeople are ripe for conversion. Yet only two missionaries are appointed as circuit ministers to spend full time on evangelism, church planting, and supervision. (See table of missionary distribution below.) Eleven missionaries, on the other hand, are appointed to devote full time to improving the social and economic conditions of the people. Admittedly, there is some overlapping. Those not appointed primarily to serve "church life" do engage in it; and those not appointed primarily to improve the physical condition of the people do engage in that. Nevertheless, the great majority of missionary time and money is directed toward benevolences. Clearly there is an imbalance.

Any study of church growth must ask what the relationship is between social service (which uses the majority of missionary funds and personnel) and church growth (which ought to be the controlling aim of missions). At Rotifunk, where there is a mission hospital, there is a static church and circuit. At Jaiama, with a hospital clinic and a secondary school, we see a static church. At Taiama, where there is a mission clinic, we see great growth, but the clinic had little or nothing to do with the growth. Where community and agricultural development has been done, we do not see any greater growth. We have seen that schools do not produce church growth, although once a church exists they may provide church leadership.

### EVANGELICAL UNITED BRETHREN CHURCH
Responsibilities of Missionary Personnel
(1965-1966)

| | | |
|---|---|---|
| Church Life | | 5 |
| Evangelism and church planting | 2* | |
| Chaplaincy at Albert Academy | 1 | |
| Strengthening local church stewardship | 1 | |
| Training evangelists (Bible school) | 1 | |
| Benevolences | | 11 |
| Medicine | 5** | |
| Teaching better farming methods | 2* | |

* One on furlough
** One on study leave

| Teaching carpentry (Bible school) | 1 | |
|---|---|---|
| Teaching in secondary school | 1 | |
| Building and maintenance | 2* | |
| Miscellaneous | | 3 |
| Field Representative | 1 | |
| Business Agent | 1 | |
| Teaching missionaries' children | 1 | |

19

This is the usual case. Joseph Wold (1968) in his study of church growth in Liberia shows that the Methodist (American) Church at Ganta has great social service in medicine and education. "But in spite of this tremendous investment and expenditure in institutions," he writes, "there has been almost no growth of the church."

This story resembles thousands of others around the world. The London Missionary Society mission to Tahiti began with a social program and obtained no converts for sixteen years. In New Zealand, also, no real advances resulted from agricultural and educational station projects until the Church Missionary Society appointed Henry Williams for the specific work of itinerant evangelism. Social service, i.e., instruction in western ways of doing things, does not yield many converts. On the contrary, it is conversion through evangelism that causes converts to appreciate social service and to benefit from it.

Missions around the world illustrate the hazards of foreign mission social service, especially when institutionalized. The dangers are (1) that social service become an end in itself, helping materially the few people around the social service centers, and (2) that it draw attention away from the primary goal of discipling peoples and planting churches. These dangers are not inevitable, but it takes concentrated effort toward church growth to avoid them.

What, then, is the place of benevolences or social service in overseas missions? From the beginning of missionary endeavor in Sierra Leone, social service — medical help, education (both academic and technical or practical), and community development — has been felt to be an integral part of evangelism. This was perhaps justified to gain a foothold in a hostile land, to gain a hearing from the antagonistic people. But now that the church is established (to a certain extent) and the people are not antagonistic, what is the place of Christian social service? How can it be used as a servant of the Church to further church growth?

To answer this, we must first discover its purposes. Its purpose is not evangelism. That is, its purpose is not the winning of people to Christ and leading them to become responsible members of His Church. It is a fruit of the Gospel, not the root. Christian social service may be considered a means of gaining a hearing, or of softening the people's attitude toward Christianity, or perhaps of showing the advantages of the Christian way of life; but it does not of itself lead people to Christ and membership in the Church, although evangelism coupled with social service may do so (McGavran 1965:9:7).

Laying these ulterior motives aside, the real purpose of Christian social service is to raise the physical level of a people or a country. Medical services help some people toward better health. Education provides the nation, the Church, and many organizations with needed literate leaders and workers. Technical training helps some people to be better employed and do higher quality work. Community development through agricultural training helps some farmers to rise out of poverty through cash crops and animal husbandry.

But Christian social service is more than just social service. It becomes Christian when it flows from a heart of love and social concern. It becomes indigenous and Christian when members of local churches are moved by the deplorable conditions of their families and fellow countrymen and seek to raise themselves out of poverty, sickness, and illiteracy to a better, happier, and freer way of life.

The purpose of missions is to plant multitudes of indigenous churches — churches which not only financially support themselves, have their own leaders, and conduct their own outreach, but also which have their own programs of Christian social service. This is one of the overlooked points in which missions have so drastically failed and pauperized the churches. In missions' efforts to raise the physical level of the people they have failed to make loving service of their neighbors an indigenous part of the local churches. Since social service is a project of foreign Christian concern, even when devolved to African control, it is limited to helping only a small number of people, because of the limited amount of money and personnel. But if it were an indigenous part of the local churches, it would be indefinitely reproducible, limited only by the number of planted local churches. The place of social service in overseas missions is, therefore, to help the people through the local churches to improve their own social conditions. How can this be done?

Eugene Nida has an excellent discussion on the relationship of mission social service to the emerging national church. In his article, "The Church and Its Ministries," he answers a letter from the mission field. The missionary problem the letter revealed was that the national church was not appreciating the social service institutions; and tension was rising between the missionaries and the nationals because the nationals thought the money spent on institutions would be better spent if it went directly toward helping local churches. In his reply Nida says:

> One of the fundamental difficulties which missions and missionaries have had through the years is distinguishing clearly between (a) the church and (b) the ministries of the church.
>
> In a normal situation the ministries of the church are derived directly from the church itself, but on the mission field the ministries are often simply those of some North American or European church, and they are frequently developed in order to produce a church rather than being produced by the church in the area in which they exist. Here lies the crux of the difficulty.
>
> In most situations the history of this conflict between the church and the ministries of the church means that the ministries come first (as an extension of the foreign church) and they are usually developed with little or no relationship to the church in the country....
>
> ... Moreover the many institutions which are involved in these special ministries ... almost inevitably require far more money than does church extension. It is not strange, therefore, that the local ministers contend that they are getting the "short end of the stick." They often feel left out, for frankly, the program is out of balance (1963:10: 233-234).

Having diagnosed the problem, Nida goes on to suggest remedial steps. One is critical evaluation of the ministries. Some may be essential to the Church, others may be significant for the sending church only as expressions of "concern for the world."

However, the fact that these ministries seemed at one time to be significant for the sending church (and the mission) does not necessarily mean that they will always prove essential or vital and that the local church should take them over. Each church must itself decide what are its own indispensable ministries.

I suggest that the ministries, or social service, of the Evangelical United Brethren Church (supported almost entirely from America) can become an integral part of the church program and be servants of the Church. For example, an Evangelical United Brethren missionary was* showing some of the larger local churches in Sierra Leone how to build economical, but permanent, chapels with their own resources. This is a recent innovation and a much needed one. This principle should be extended to medical services. It will be difficult because the people have learned to depend upon the mission or government for medical aid. They feel that if they are unable to travel the distance, they must go without help. Government and mission hospitals are swamped with cases which could be handled through simple hygiene or preventive medicine. Let the local churches be taught to arrange local clinics to handle these cases and teach hygiene. Let the hospitals be used for serious cases.

Besides this, Christian hospitals offer a unique opportunity for evangelism. Because there is no follow-up, preaching services at the Evangelical United Brethren hospitals and clinics are almost valueless. But if they were followed up, greater church growth would likely occur.

Gordon Robinson, a missionary to Nigeria, reported the church growth effect of a Baptist hospital in southern Nigeria.

This hospital has an intensive regular evangelistic program with a careful follow-up program. (a) The Gospel is preached daily to every patient with the objective of bringing him to a definite decision for Christ. (b) Evangelism is the planned responsibility of every member of the staff. (c) Religious records are kept on each patient and all decisions are re-

* This missionary returned permanently to America in 1968.

corded. (d) Information on each decision is sent to the church nearest the patient's home when he is discharged from the hospital. (e) One or two days a week the chaplain makes field trips to visit former patients in their villages to see whether they have followed through their decision and are active in a church. (f) Most of the senior staff members of the hospital (including the doctors) have regular itinerant responsibilities in the churches of the areas around the hospital.

This program has been carefully worked out to bring the influence of the hospital to bear in the greatest possible degree upon planting and growing churches (Grimley and Robinson: 1966, 361-362).

This principle of making Christian social service indigenous to the local churches should also be applied to community development. The program as structured belongs properly in the sphere of government, and is considered by the nationals to have little to do with the Church, although its value as help to the nation is appreciated. The greatest value to the Church of community development missionaries now appears to nationals to be their secondary activities as evangelists.

But community development through foreign missions can and ought to be fully related to the Church. Its primary concern should not be to teach better farming and animal husbandry directly to "the public" and thus raise its standard of living, but to assist local churches to raise themselves and their villages by showing them how they can increase their income.

Perhaps this can be done by operating a mission-run "ideal" farm, but such a farm has dangers. It tempts the missionary who runs it (1) to limit his help to those who live nearby, whether they be of the local church or not, and (2) to purchase and use equipment which the poor village farmer cannot afford. The government has many fine programs of community development and agricultural improvement, but few villages are profiting by them. The local churches might be better helped if they were shown how to use existing government aid. This means mobility on the part of the missionaries charged with this responsibility.

Social service through overseas missions ought to be the servant of the national Church. When in reality it is, it strengthens the Church and helps the greatest number of people. However, as important and as helpful as social service is, it is no substitute for the primary aim of missions, which is evangelism geared to multiplying local churches. This primary aim should receive the largest portion of missionary personnel and funds.

# CHAPTER II

# THE UNITED BRETHREN IN CHRIST CHURCH

## ORGANIZATIONAL STRUCTURE

The United Brethren in Christ in Sierra Leone (comprising a Christian community of about three thousand) are well organized, with an adequate supply of ordained ministers. The Conference is divided into four districts, each having a part-time conference superintendent, i.e., the superintendent is pastor of his own church as well as supervisor of his district. Three of the districts are in the comity area (see map on page 71), and the fourth comprises churches on Sherbro Island and in and around Freetown. Each district is small enough to allow for adequate supervision. The superintendent holds a quarterly conference in each *charge,* i.e., each circuit or station.

Each district is divided into circuits or stations. A circuit consists of two to four organized societies under one minister. A station is one organized society under a minister. Besides this, each organized society may have one or two preaching points which the minister is to visit weekly. Enough men are ordained to provide adequately for the sacraments.

The Church has three categories of paid preachers: one is licensed at quarterly conference within the local church, another at the annual session of Conference, and the third ordained by Conference. Most are Class III leaders, i.e., they serve small churches and receive small salaries. The ordained men, most of whom are Class III leaders and a few Class IV, comprise the majority of the paid preachers. Only the ordained may serve the sacraments. Four years in the conference reading course or three years in the Bible college qualifies a candidate for ordination.

With respect to devolution, one hospital and two dispensaries are still in stage one. They are controlled jointly by missionaries and nationals and are directly responsible to the home board in America. Two secondary schools are controlled by the government. Church life and evangelism are in stage two. Conference has been administered by nationals since 1964. A council of missionaries meets regularly, but there is no joint council in which representatives of both groups meet together.

*No evangelistic missionaries are actively engaged in church planting.* One missionary teaches in the newly opened (1965) Sierra Leone Bible College near Freetown, a joint school serving the United Brethren in Christ, the American Wesleyan Methodists, and any other Church caring to participate. Another missionary is secretary of Christian education and prepares Sunday School lessons for the churches.

## CHURCH GROWTH

The question of church growth in the United Brethren in Christ Church is especially pertinent because this Church has ordained Class III leaders. Does ordaining these leaders produce growth?

The graph on page 74 compares growth in the tribal Churches. The United Brethren in Christ Church is stagnating. From the beginning the school approach was used and stations were begun by opening schools. Later, churches emerged. The membership statistics of the local churches show that none has ever broken away from its school to begin an ingathering of tribespeople.* In the churches I visited (four near Mattru, two being former Methodist Churches which changed because of comity agreement), growth is mainly among school children, and most of the Christians are of the second or third generation. The graph on page 74 indicates that the United Brethren in Christ doubled their membership from 1950 to 1960. But the growth is the result of opening numerous stations and schools. Usually, when a school-church opens, a small, static Christian community emerges. This pattern does not win the populace to Christ.

The area is strongly Muslim although mostly nominal,

* Statistics of individual local churches are available only from 1945 to 1957.

and animists are still plentiful. The Christians live with them in peaceful coexistence. The preacher pastors his tiny group of Christians and does not itinerate, except to his one or two preaching points.* The records do not indicate how responsive or resistant the people are to Christianity. Perhaps no consistent attempt has been made to win the populace, thereby discovering the people's readiness to turn to Christ.

Ordination of Class III leaders in itself does not result in church growth, although such ordination is necessary for effective pastoring. Itinerating to proclaim Christ, to win people to Him, to plant village congregations, and to follow up with training local leaders often produces church growth. The two should be combined. The United Brethren in Christ need to send out church planters.

* In 1965 there were forty-eight stations, some recently opened. The minutes of the annual sessions indicate that what is true of the area I visited is generally true of the whole Conference.

# CHAPTER 12

# THE AMERICAN WESLEYAN
# METHODIST CHURCH*

The American Wesleyan Methodist Mission in Sierra Leone had a tremendous strategy. It planned to stop the spread of Islam. The reasons for its limited success and general failure in stopping Islam (by 1965 the Church had an adult Christian community of only 5,600) apply to most mission fields of the world. Today some of the mistakes of the past are being rectified through the use of vernacular-trained pastors.

## BEGINNINGS

The American Wesleyan Church entered Sierra Leone, its first mission field, in 1889. The northern area was chosen (see the comity map on page 71) for several reasons. (1) J. A. Cole, a relative of a Limba paramount chief, requested the American Wesleyan Methodists to come. He was an educated Limba and a member of St. John's Church in Freetown. (2) Few missionary societies had ventured beyond the coast. (3) The interior tribes offered opportunities for missionary work superior to those located on the coast because the effects of the old slave trade, of the liquor traffic, and of evil European influence were less, and the people governed themselves.

The General Conference in America ordained Mr. Cole and sent their first missionary, Rev. A. W. Hall, to found a mission station. After Hall arrived in Sierra Leone (April 11, 1889) he negotiated with the officials of St. John's Church

---

* Most of the information regarding this Church is from *A Half Century of American Wesleyan Missions in West Africa* (Carter 1946) unless otherwise noted.

CHURCHES IN CENTRAL AND
NORTH SIERRA LEONE

GUINEA

SUSU

YALUNKA

△ Bafodia

Kabala °

° Bendugu

Kamakwie

Kukuna

TEMNE

LIMBA

LIMBA

△ American Wesleyan Meth.
○ Missionary Church Assn.
▽ Seventh Day Adventist
□ Evangelical United Breth.
🗹 E.U.B. & S.D.A.
🅜 E.U.B., S.D.A. & M.C.A.

LOKO

Gbendembu

Kamabai

Batkanu △

△ Binkolo

KORANKO

Makeni

Magburaka

K
O
N
O

TEMNE

○ Mayaso

TEMNE

Petifu

Mondema □

Yonibana

Yele ▽

□ Mongere

Rotifunk □

Taiama □

Moyamba

Dambara

MENDE

Mano

MENDE

Bo

to make their church a member of the Wesleyan Methodist Connection of America, and a child of the Parent Missionary Society. Then he and Cole went to Limbaland, 150 miles from the coast, to begin missionary work. Kunso Chiefdom* was chosen because it was almost equally divided in population among the representatives of three tribes: Temne, Limba, and Loko. Within twelve years (by 1910) seven mission stations were opened and staffed by thirteen missionaries.

## METHOD OF EVANGELISM

The method of evangelism used was a combination of schools, medical work, and wide itineration to "bring the Gospel" to as many villages as possible. In 1930, for example, nine hundred towns were reached, 462 people were converted, and 319 of them joined the Church. The work, however, was heavily dependent upon missionary personnel and funds. Mission stations and outstations opened and closed as missionary personnel were made available or withdrawn.

The story of Kamakwie illustrates this dependency (see the map on preceding page). The people of Kamakwie were resentful of Christianity until a respected man, healed at Mobai by a missionary doctor, returned home. All were surprised to see him alive, and were then ready to listen to the Gospel. Having established Christianity in Kamakwie, the missionaries proceeded in a program to check Islam from spreading southward from Susuland. They planted a line of outstations, running from east to west, staffed by native workers under the supervision of the missionary at Kamakwie. The evangelists were to spend twenty days of each month away from their stations visiting and evangelizing the towns and villages surrounding Kamakwie.

After five years of pioneer evangelism, the mission station at Kamakwie was closed because of an insufficiency of funds and missionaries to maintain all the stations of the Mission. The missionary at Kamakwie was transferred to the boys' school at Binkolo. In the absence of resident missionaries the native workers became discouraged and careless, and the people lost interest.

* There is no chiefdom by this name at the present time.

Added to this the chief at Kamakwie, who had been favorable to Christianity, died. In his place, following occasional custom, a non-Limba Muslim chief was crowned, who in turn crowned foreign Muslim subchiefs. Two of the outstations were closed. Carter, the Mission's historian, concluded as a result of the aforementioned situation,

> Almost every barrier that had once been constructed against the influx of Mohammedans was removed. Thus did Mohammedanism in the presence of a depleted mission work and a pro-Mohammedan ruler avail itself of the opportunity to invade the Sella land that had once offered such bright prospects to the Christian Missions (1946).

No real barriers, however, had been constructed. Mere planting of mission stations and outstations, placement of paid workers, and evangelism do not constitute a barrier to anything. All these are simply the wires in a sieve through which water flows easily. A barrier to Islam is not erected until people are converted and churches are planted throughout the villages of the land. Multiplying churches stop up the holes of a sieve. The people of Sierra Leone are changing from animism to something. They are ripe for change. Many are becoming Muslim. The trend toward Islam can be stopped only when one toward Christianity is established. Such a trend will occur only when many villagers in each village turn to Christ and churches are multiplied throughout the land.

Usually it takes several years for a people newly introduced to Christianity to understand it well enough to be convinced of its truth and thereby be ripe for conversion. In the Evangelical United Brethren Mondema Parish, two years of constant itinerating among the villages to proclaim Christ passed before the people were ripe for conversion. For the people of Mondema, Christianity was not new; they had heard about it for possibly three generations. But the message of salvation through Christ was new. They had never heard the Gospel preached before, and it took two years to produce a people movement.

The American Wesleyan Methodists at Kamakwie, beginning in 1919, had only five years in which to proclaim salvation through Christ. Since Christianity was totally new to the people, five years probably was not sufficient time in which to bring the people to conversion. So a barrier against Islam had not been erected, although sowers of the Gospel had walked through the land.

One wonders whether it was wise on the part of the Mission to transfer the missionary from Kamakwie to the boys' school at Binkolo. This incident shows one way in which social service institutions may halt church growth. Evangelism and church planting suffer first from a shortage of missionaries and funds because continuity in institutions, where much money is invested, is considered more important. The reverse ought to prevail. Institutions should be short staffed in favor of church planting, which is the primary goal of missions.

## A PEOPLE MOVEMENT STOPPED

The wide itinerating of missionaries and paid workers around 1930 produced a "revival." Several churches were born and some existing churches strengthened. At Robing, a Temne town, "almost the entire town and many people of the surrounding country forsook heathenism, were transformed by the power of God and became definitely Christian" (Carter: 1946). The description sounds as though a people movement were beginning. But it was short lived.

At first glance one reason for the stoppage would seem to be an uprising nearby in the following year. A Muslim prophet from French West Africa organized an uprising against the government and Christianity. Several churches suffered. In one town the Muslim demonstration and threats of destruction or expulsion of Christians, as well as of government personnel, scattered the flock and almost ruined the church. The uprising was quickly put down when the prophet and some of his followers were killed in the first skirmish. Yet Robing was not mentioned as one of the churches which suffered directly from the uprising.

Lack of follow-up to encourage the people movement until the whole tribe (Temne) was won, or at least a large segment of the tribe, probably is a major reason for the end of the small spurt at Robing. Supervising missionaries and their national successors usually consider all outstations equal, whether or not churches at the outstations are growing, and whether or not village congregations around the outstations are being planted. Thus an evangelist blessed with a responsiveness around his outstation too big for him to handle must expect no help, because all the other evangelists have their own tiny congregations to pastor, and "maybe their surrounding villagers will become responsive." To transfer an evangelist from a seemingly nonresponsive outstation to help another evangelist harvest a people movement would be a disservice to the struggling, heavily dependent outstation church and to the surrounding villages. The tiny congregation might collapse. This is the argument given against transferring evangelists from nonresponsive to responsive areas.

Meanwhile, the people movement of the one evangelist is not followed up in such a way as to bring the maximum numbers of souls to Christ, and the tiny congregation of the other evangelist remains tiny. This is what happened at Mongere of the Evangelical United Brethren Church. It is probably the main reason why it happened at Robing. Thirty-five years after the beginning of the people movement at Robing only thirty-eight full members, 209 associate members (baptized but not permitted to partake of communion or hold office, similar to the Methodist classification of members on trial), and nineteen catechumens preparing for baptism were found in four surrounding towns which were receiving regular evangelistic visits. Had there been a conscious effort to multiply self-propagating village congregations, the story might have resembled that of Taiama, of the Evangelical United Brethren Church. As it is, all we have is an arrested people movement — a common, though usually unrecognized, occurrence in mission history.

## ORGANIZATIONAL STRUCTURE

Missionaries supervised the planted outstations in the early period. This was stage one of devolution. Later, the churches were divided into quarterly conferences, each with an ordained African pastor as supervisor, one of whom was elected Conference Superintendent. The missionary evangelists became unofficial supervisors of the churches, but remained school managers; and the mission superintendent, remaining as conference president, chaired the annual session of the Conference and wielded the authority. In 1958 one of the minister supervisors was elected full-time conference president, the mission superintendent then becoming an advisor — producing stage two in church life.

In 1965 the Church had thirty-five churches — twenty-four organized and eleven unorganized. These, plus a hospital, were staffed by five kinds of paid leaders:

| Paid Leaders | NUMBER |
|---|---|
| Teacher-agent | 1 |
| Lay itinerator | 2 |
| Unordained vernacular-trained* pastor | 19 |
| Unordained English-trained** pastor | 9 |
| Ordained minister | 5 |
| | — |
| | 36 |

The Conference is self-supporting. Some pastors are on full local support, and those who are not receive their entire support from the Conference. The Conference receives the money for this by levying all the churches.

Vernacular and English pastor training schools serve the Church. The one in English had operated alone until 1961, but closed in that year because the students came only to acquire more education to enable them to pass examinations to enter secondary school or teacher training college. Since the school was no longer serving the Church, it was changed into a vernacular school. In 1965 the Sierra Leone Bible College was opened near Freetown in cooperation with the United Brethren in Christ.

The vernacular school is structured to serve the Church. It has a four-year program with three terms in each year. Two terms are spent at the school, and the third is spent in intensive village evangelism. Sixteen students graduated after four years of operation and were stationed in those villages which showed the most response to the periods of intensive evangelism. The statistics for their churches are encouraging, showing many are interested in Christianity.

Eleven outstations have been opened since 1960. One is served by a lay itinerator (untrained but soon to be trained), one by an evangelist graduated from the defunct English Bible

* Trained four years in a vernacular Bible school.
** Trained four years in an English Bible school.

school, and the rest served by evangelists who have been trained two to four years at the vernacular Bible school. At these eleven churches there were, in 1965, 256 catechumens, 993 persons seeking Christ (that is, showing interest in Christianity), and 382 professed conversions.

The church organization, method of supervision (I am informed that supervision is almost nil), and method of training are buttressed by a missionary staff whose assignments are arranged as follows (1965):

*Church Life*                                                    4
    Evangelism and church planting
      (with dispensary)                              2
    Print shop, radio station, vernacular
      Bible school                                   2
*Benevolences*                                                  14
    Girls' boarding school and dispensary     2
    Other schools                                  4
    Hospital                                       7
    Field engineer                                 1
*Miscellaneous*                                                  1
    Nurse for missionaries' children's
      boarding school                            1
                                         —
                                        19

## CHURCH GROWTH

The American Wesleyan Methodist Church experienced moderate growth (see the graph on page 74) and no continuing people movements. Devolution in "church life" has not yielded any greater statistical growth during the seven years since 1958, when an African became conference president. Taking three seven-year periods, the growth percentages are as follows:

| Years | Chairmanship | Seven-Year Increase | |
|---|---|---|---|
| | | numbers | percentage |
| 1944-1951 | Mission | 22 | 1.8% |
| 1951-1958 | Mission | 798 | 65.0% |
| 1958-1965 | African | 666 | 32.9% |

This implies that not devolution alone, but a change in evangelistic methods, is required to produce church growth.

It is too early to see results from the new outstations

opened by vernacular-trained pastors. If, however, the Gospel is presented in such a way as to encourage whole families and whole villages to turn to Christ, if conversions are followed up by planting village congregations and training local leaders, and if the sacraments are made an integral part of the program to multiply churches, then we may expect people movements to occur and churches to multiply. The African pastors, not being tied down to school management, ought to be more free to plant churches and give adequate supervision than are the Evangelical United Brethren ministers.

Churches in Sierra Leone, confronting a two-level society, need leaders trained to serve on each level. When the need for vernacular-trained leadership was recognized, Conference wisely opened a vernacular Bible school. The Methodists also have such a school, but the Evangelical United Brethren and the United Brethren in Christ have not, and thus do not have vernacular-trained leaders to work in the villages among the tribal people. However, the American Wesleyan Methodists have no adequate training program for producing leaders educated for the higher level. The four-year English Bible school did not meet this need. Hopefully the newly opened Sierra Leone Bible College near Freetown will.

# CHAPTER 13

# SEVENTH-DAY ADVENTIST CHURCH*

The Seventh-day Adventists began mission work in Sierra Leone in 1907. For fifty-two years, until 1959, they experienced very slow growth. From 1959 to 1963 the membership doubled, rising from 1017 to 2054 in four years (see graph on page 74). Whether the Seventh-day Adventists will continue to double every four years remains to be seen. However, their tight organization, with close supervision, equips them to make plans for church growth and to carry them out.

Whether they multiply churches or not will depend on how well they consider and apply the many factors mentioned in this book. The increase of 102 per cent in four years looks as if they have found responsiveness in some place or places. The map on page 178 shows where most of their churches are located. If they regard the growing churches as God's gift and push on to vigorous church planting, the next decade might see notable growth. God grant that they act in time, for Christians in Sierra Leone do not have many years of opportunity before them.

A summary of their present organizational structure on the following page shows their method of church planting. Conference headquarters handles all finances. Each local church has a local fund to pay for Sabbath School materials and to cover maintenance costs of the Church, and sends the tithes and offerings (Sabbath School offerings, church offerings, special project offerings) to the mission treasurer and secretary, who pays all workers' and pastors' salaries. Regardless of the size of the church, each worker (depending on his rank in

---

* The information for this chapter is from an interview with Pastor Christensen, president of the Seventh-day Adventist Mission, 1964.

the ministry) gets the same salary. The Seventh-day Adventists
have a very thorough stewardship program.

SEVENTH-DAY ADVENTIST CHURCH
Organizational Structure

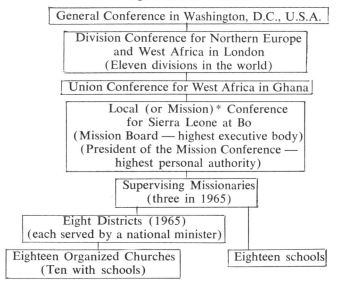

The Church has four levels of leadership. The first level
(Class I leaders) consists of unpaid, ordained church elders.
They are found in every organized church, and they are responsible for conducting funerals and church services. Leaders
on the next three levels are paid: evangelists, licensed ministers in training for ordination (only four ·of these in Sierra
Leone), and ordained ministers (only eleven in Sierra Leone
— three European and eight African). African ministers are
trained in Nigeria. Every month all eight district pastors come
to Bo to (1) receive salaries for themselves and their evangelists and teachers, (2) give tithes and offerings, and (3)
have a one-day inspirational meeting. The institute, from year
to year, varies in the groups of persons it seeks to train; e.g.,
ministers, ministers' wives, teachers, or licensed ministers.

* A Local Conference is called a Mission Conference until it is
self-supporting.

A church member passes through four levels of church relationship. The first is Sabbath School attender. The Sabbath School is the main thrust of evangelism and is the recruiting place for the hearers' class, which is the next level. Every Sabbath (Saturday), teachers, evangelists, and ministers itinerate through the villages conducting Sabbath School classes. The lesson material used for each Sabbath is the same used all over the world for that day. Instruction in these classes forms the heart of evangelistic endeavor and of church services. It would be better, however, if the materials used were adapted to the African culture.

The next two levels form a catechism class. One year is spent in the hearers' class and one in the probationers' class. To remain in good standing in these classes one must obey the many laws of the Seventh-day Adventist Church, particularly regarding monogamy and nonmembership in secret societies. After this comes the fourth level — baptism and full membership.

The tight organization of the Seventh-day Adventist Church, if directed toward church growth, may well yield church multiplication.

# CHAPTER 14

# THE ASSEMBLIES OF GOD CHURCH*

## METHOD AND CONDITIONS OF CHURCH GROWTH

The mission work of the Assemblies of God Church among the Kissi at Koindu (see the people movement map on page 119) began upon invitation. Fourteen miles across the border at Foya, in Liberia, the Swedish Pentecostal Mission had a station. In 1952 evangelists from the station began preaching around Koindu among their own tribesmen. On their second visit four young men gave themselves to Christ and then began going to Foya every Sunday. They went for three years, their numbers increasing as they brought others with them. They also began preaching in the villages around Koindu, winning many to Christ.

An old man in one village, the home of one of the young men, directed persecution against the Christians. He often had the young men beaten, and when Christians gathered poles with which to build a chapel, he would cut the poles for firewood. Despite this, the chapel was built. Even then, the old man, who lived next to the chapel, would make loud noises during services. But the Christians persevered. Then one day the old man became sick. Neither his own "medicine" nor European medicine helped. Finally he asked God for help and for the Christians to pray for him. God healed him, and he left his old ways, burned all his "medicines," and gave his life to Jesus.

This was not the only instance of persecution. The high moral demands and the definite break with the old ways, including polygamy, secret society membership, and Sunday marketing, generated general persecution of Christians. This has yielded a strong church and has impressed upon the

* Interview with Mr. Jonathan Glover, 1965.

tribespeople that to become Christian means not just the taking of a name, but *giving* their lives to God. Today, now that Christianity is more accepted, persecution has ceased.

In 1955 the Swedish Pentecostal Mission tried to establish a mission station at Koindu, but the Sierra Leone government refused, not wanting another mission body to be added to the many already in the country. The Christians at Koindu were then directed to the Assemblies of God missionaries in Freetown who were working among the Kru immigrants from Liberia. To help the Christians around Koindu, a missionary visited twice a year to preach and teach. This continued until 1961.

In 1961 a missionary stayed for six months, preaching in the villages, helping the people construct a church building, and building a mission residence. In 1962 a man and his wife were sent as resident evangelistic missionaries. They were to organize the Church and begin a Bible school in which to train the church leaders for church work and ordination.

The Bible school began in 1963 with an enrollment of forty men. The requirements for attendance were: the student must (1) not be in debt, (2) have no more than one wife, (3) have been baptized with water, (4) have been baptized with the Holy Spirit or be seeking such baptism, (5) be a member of a church or in the process of becoming a member, (6) attend church regularly, (7) be willing to abide by all the rules and regulations of the Bible school, (8) provide for his own food and textbooks, and (9) understand that if he is accepted he is not promised or guaranteed an appointment upon completion of the course.

Because the students earn their support as farmers, the school operates in the morning during harvest season and until brushing time for the next year's farm. An oil palm plantation has been started to provide income for students so they can attend school for two terms each year instead of one. The school is conducted in English because there is no literature available in the Kissi language. The curriculum includes English, arithmetic and record keeping, Bible studies, and doctrine.

Within six and one-half miles of Koindu, in 1964, there

were twenty-nine village congregations, six of which were organized. One village congregation was eleven miles away. These were served by eighteen voluntary workers, all preparing for ordination at the Bible school. Services in the villages are held on Friday. The Christians of the villages are expected to come to Koindu Sunday morning for Sunday School and church services.

The Sunday School is divided into five classes — three for children and two for adults. The classes are taught by Kissi who receive instruction from the missionary on Saturday afternoon. The Sunday School pattern of instruction includes two lessons, one recapitulation and the other new. The teachers use large Bible pictures and flannelgraphs. Although most of them are nonliterate, they quickly learn how to use such material and are effective teachers.

The requirements for baptism are high. The candidate must learn the catechism, which includes doctrine and lessons on Christian living. To learn the catechism, a five-day, two-hour-per-day course is given and regular attendance is required. Besides this, each candidate must give one-tenth of his income to the church. Moral requirements include monogamy and abstention from alcohol, smoking, secret society membership, and Sunday marketing. Society membership is prohibited because of non-Christian practices which are part of societies and because a Christian's allegiance should be to God only. Sunday marketing is prohibited because Sunday is the Lord's Day. Yet Sunday is the day in which traders from all three countries — Sierra Leone, Liberia, and Guinea — come to Koindu. Thus it is the day of greatest opportunity for earning money. To obey this law is a real sacrifice on the part of the Christian.

Discipline forms a significant part of church life. Offenders of church laws are called before the elders of the congregation and are sentenced to sit on the bench at the back of the chapel. That is, the missionaries have taught the rules of the Church so well that the congregational leaders believe in them and therefore enforce them.

The preachers emphasize salvation, winning others, prayer, and healing. Every service ends with an altar call for those who desire to be saved, to be healed, or to commit themselves more fully to God. During the services all singing is accompanied by percussion instruments (drums and shake shakes) and clapping.

## CHURCH GROWTH

Despite the high standards of Christianity, perhaps even because of them, the number of Christians has grown. Christians are classified into two categories — active adult members, and other believers. In an effort to be conservative, statistics for the latter were recorded by the missionaries as half of what the volunteer preachers reported. Below is a table showing the growth.*

| Year | Active Members | Other Believers | Other Believers Doubled | Total Adult Christian Community |
|---|---|---|---|---|
| 1962 | 80 | 56 | 112 | 192 |
| 1963 | 83 | 193 | 386 | 469 |
| 1964 | 83 | 294 | 588 | 671 |

The period is too short for definite appraisal, yet this much is clear: Although the number of Christians has greatly increased, the number of those who meet the requirements to be considered active has not. This is in keeping with the policy of the Assemblies of God Church.

## LESSONS FOR OTHER CHURCHES

Several aspects of the Assemblies of God program ought to be emphasized, which, if adopted by other Churches in Sierra Leone, would yield greater growth and stronger churches.

(1) A complete break with the past through the burning of medicines and charms. This is a symbol of complete rejection of the old way and of complete dependence upon God through Christ and the Holy Spirit. In all the Churches of Sierra Leone, members are prohibited from using charms or making sacrifices. But often members comply by word of mouth only, and yield to the pressures of family to protect their

* The graph on page 74 showing the growth of the Assemblies of God Church combines the memberships of the Kissi Church at Koindu for 1965 and the Kru Church in Freetown. Statistics for the former are taken from station records at Koindu. Those for the latter are from the *World Christian Handbook* for 1962.

children by the use of charms. As a result, many "Christians" believe both in Christ and in the power of charms. This leads to syncretism. There needs to be a complete, formal, public break with the old way.

(2) Faith in the power of God to heal. This is an integral part of the Assemblies of God Church. It is almost wholly lacking in the other Churches. Because of this, many Christians still use magical charms and "medicine." Church is merely a Sunday affair. Christianity is not relevant for their whole life. The Assemblies of God pray for those desiring healing through the laying on of hands. Some are healed, others are not. But the Christians have a firm belief in the power of God in their lives.

(3) Holy Spirit baptism. This usually implies speaking ecstatically in tongues. But it also means complete submission of the will to God and the receiving of God's power and guidance, which results in holy living and in zealous evangelism and soul winning. This zeal was evident in the lives of the Christians at Koindu. With a few notable exceptions, I found it wholly lacking in the lives of Christians elsewhere — both leaders and followers. Many Christians seem merely to have become church people. They bear the name of Christ but do not possess His power. One reason for this is the almost total lack of instruction concerning the Holy Spirit. The Churches and Christians of Sierra Leone need revival and Holy Spirit baptism.

(4) Enthusiastic worship, using clapping, drums, and shake shakes, in which all participate. Two things which have most harmed worship services in the churches of Sierra Leone are dead singing and nonparticipation of worshippers.

(5) Training and using Sunday School teachers from among the nonliterate tribespeople. This builds up indigenous leadership.

(6) Pastors not supported by foreign funds. They supplement their income by farming until the local churches can support them.

(7) Source of leadership from the local churches. The leaders are thus proved, mature men; not immature, westernized schoolboys.

(8) Church discipline maintained by the church members themselves. In some other Churches the missionaries and national supervisors have become as policemen enforcing rules, thus militating against the emergence of local church responsibility. However, the rules local church leaders are taught to enforce ought to be based on Grace and not Law. Enforced high standards, regardless of the source, lead to legalism.

# CHAPTER 15

# THE MISSIONARY CHURCH ASSOCIATION*

The first missionaries of the Missionary Church Association who came to Sierra Leone did not intend to establish a separate Church. Rather, they intended to establish congregations and then turn them over to other Churches. When they got too far into the interior, however (see the map on page 178 for the location of some of their churches), other Churches were not willing to accept, staff, and supervise the congregations. Therefore, the Missionary Church Association began a new denomination.

The school approach was not used. Instead, the national workers were trained in the vernacular. This policy was followed so that students would not be tempted to leave the area for the big towns and other work and thus no longer be of service to the Church. The plan, therefore, was to make education the servant of the Church.

By 1955 the members were complaining that their Mission was not providing their children with education as the other Missions were. Yielding to the pressure, the Mission opened a school in 1955. By 1962 ten schools were open, with an enrollment of 713 students. Also by 1962, 219 baptized members in good standing were distributed among eight organized churches and nineteen regular meeting centers and were served by fifteen national workers, none of them ordained. The graph on page 74 shows the good growth.

This initial growth may be secured by almost any Mission which opens schools, hires teachers, and baptizes school children and other converts. It is usually hothouse growth and does not continue. The school approach seals off the general

* Interview with Mr. Kenneth Rupp, 1962.

populace. The graph (p. 74) shows that growth is already slowing down.

In view of the Mission's initial purpose to use education as the servant of the Church, the Missionary Church Association may avoid stagnation by using the schools as spring boards for vigorous itineration with the purpose of winning families and larger social units to Christ and His Church.

# CHAPTER 16

# THE NIGERIAN BAPTIST CONVENTION*

A Baptist Convention (a denomination) in America made a survey of Sierra Leone and discovered that the interior had no Baptist churches. Through the indigenous Nigerian Baptist Convention it arranged to send and support a missionary to establish the Baptist Church in Sierra Leone. The Church began in 1960 with a single congregation in an area near Magburaka where no other Protestants were working. By 1962 the church had an average attendance of seventy, but no baptized members. The people want the Nigerian missionary to open a school, but the proximity of a Roman Catholic school prohibits it.

The situation calls for the application of the indigenous approach in which local church leaders are given more authority and in which the Christians participate in village evangelism and church planting.

* Interview with Rev. F. Boya, 1962.

# CHAPTER 17

# INDIGENOUS CHURCHES

## GOD IS OUR LIGHT CHURCH*

This indigenous Church, with headquarters for Sierra Leone in Freetown, began in Ghana. The Church has no sacraments. Membership is based on regular attendance, baptism of the Holy Spirit, and observance of the laws. One of the laws prohibits going to doctors or using medicine (European, pagan, or Muslim). For healing one must depend solely upon the laying on of hands in prayer. Another law, reversing the order of most Churches in Sierra Leone, prohibits membership in secret societies but permits polygamy. The church leaders feel that membership in secret societies is more damaging to the Christian life than is polygamy.

The Church, although indigenous to Ghana, is not indigenous to Sierra Leone; it is controlled from Ghana. For a church to become "recognized" with a leader, the name and qualifications of the prospective leader must be sent to Ghana, where the decision is made. Only a few God Is Our Light churches are in Sierra Leone. One of them is at Kayima in Konoland, where an Evangelical United Brethren school is located. The membership there is about forty, although the attendance is greater. The church has morning and evening prayers every day.

The Church has no missionary program with goals of winning peoples or tribes to Christ. Its spread depends upon members who settle in towns and begin worship services.

## THE CHURCH OF THE LORD (ALADURA)**

In 1947 the first Church of the Lord missionary came to

* Interviews with the church leader at Kayima plus several other informants who are familiar with the Church.
** Interviews with a Disciple, a village congregation in Taiama Parish,

198

Sierra Leone from Nigeria, where the Church originated. His name was Adejobi, and in Sierra Leone the people call the Church after his name — Adejobi Church. In 1963 the Church had twenty-six "praying groups" (*aladura* means praying group) or congregations.

The influence of the Church is quite widespread. One of the village congregations on the border of Taiama Parish began under the preaching of a "prophet" (the popular name applied to all members of the Church of the Lord in Sierra Leone) from Bo. After being neglected by the prophet for a few years, the congregation joined Taiama Parish. A woman was converted in a Church of the Lord congregation near Moyamba, and there learned how to conduct services. Upon returning to her home near Mondema she became a village congregation leader in the Evangelical United Brethren Church.

The Church of the Lord is Pentecostal, with emphasis on ecstatic experiences (Holy Spirit baptism) and faith healing. Certain rites, however, border on syncretism, i.e., combine Christian elements with animistic ones. In Sierra Leone the sacraments have little importance, "holy water" all but replacing them. This is due to the fact that of the twelve levels of ordained ministers, only the top seven may administer the sacraments. Sierra Leone has only three ministers in the top seven levels.

Ministers of all levels, however, may consecrate water. Holy water is used to perform ablutions (washing of hands and feet) before entering a place of worship and is used extensively in healing. Members bring bottles to church to be filled with holy water in the same manner as most people in Sierra Leone bring bottles to hospitals or dispensaries for medicine. The water, however, is officially not considered magical. Instead, it symbolizes faith in Jesus, who is the living water.

Other features of worship are: removal of shoes before entering church; numerous candles, which symbolize Jesus, the light of the world; incense wafted up and down the aisles from a censer, which symbolizes prayers going up before God;

and a woman leader in Mondema Circuit, and observation of a healing service in Freetown supplied information in this section.

handclapping, bells, drumming, and stationary dancing; and interpretation of visions, i.e., prophecy.

In 1963 a "Disciple" (the technical term for the first of the twelve ministerial levels) went to Kayima in Konoland "under guidance by God" to plant a church. The God Is Our Light Church had been there since 1960. At first the Disciple and those who attended his services were opposed by all the Evangelical United Brethren people, most of whom were no longer attending church, and the God Is Our Light people. (An exception was one of the schoolteachers.) However, success has caused them to be accepted. After one year they had between 150 and 200 members. Morning and evening prayers with much music and dancing are held every day in addition to Sunday worship services.

The members engage in three kinds of sacrifices — church offerings, offerings for special occasions, and almsgiving. Church offerings are turned over to the district ministers to be distributed among them, such monies being their only salary. The Disciples in the outlying villages, however, receive no salary, but are dependent upon almsgiving.

In common with the Assemblies of God, the Church of the Lord is providing for the emotional and spiritual healing needs of its members, as well as for their other spiritual needs. However, the members do not appear as missionary as do the members of the Assemblies of God. The members need to be more involved in the expansion of Christianity to other villages.

# CHAPTER 18

# THE ROMAN CATHOLIC CHURCH

The Portuguese Jesuits attempted to establish Roman Catholic Christianity in Sierra Leone during the period of Portuguese ascendancy (latter part of the fifteenth century to the latter part of the seventeenth century), but failed. In 1823 the foundress of the Sisters of St. Joseph tried and failed.

In 1858 the Fathers of the Holy Ghost set up the vicariate apostolic of Sierra Leone, which included French Guinea and Liberia. The following year a severe yellow fever epidemic killed all five of the missionaries. In 1864 the Fathers tried again; and the following year the missionary in charge reported fifteen Protestants received into the Roman Catholic Church.

In 1950 the Diocese of Freetown and Bo was established and declared directly subject to the Holy See. In 1963 there were two ecclesiastical districts with a total Roman Catholic community of 26,602 (1.2 per cent of the total population and 25 per cent of the total Christian population), plus 24,970 catechumens (Emmerich 1965: 14-15). (Compare the Roman Catholic community figure with the Protestant ones on page 72.)

The Roman Catholic Church depends heavily and almost exclusively upon the school approach. In 1963 it administered 1192 primary schools — eleven less than all the Protestant Churches cooperating in the United Christian Council combined, and a little more than one-third (35.8 per cent) of all the primary schools in Sierra Leone (Ministry of Education 1965). The emphasis being on schools, it is from schools that the Church receives most of its converts, and they are few compared with the number of schools. Each primary school has an average of only twenty-two Catholics (community). Adding in the catechumens raises the number to forty-three.

The Roman Catholics are achieving their growth through their numerous schools and are not winning the tribespeople. It is my observation that they are not even trying to do this. They open schools as fast as they can. Teachers are recruited from every source, including teachers expelled from Protestant schools on grounds of drunkenness or immorality. All that is required of them is to teach the catechism to the students and lead them in saying rosary every evening.

The government forbids compulsory attendance at worship services and compulsory learning of the catechism as requirements to pass from one class to the next. But the Roman Catholics often disregard the law. Protestant families in towns in which the only school is Roman Catholic, therefore, are often forced to see their children become Roman Catholic; for example, the families of the Nigerian Baptist Convention church near Magburaka and many Evangelical United Brethren families. In some cases, however, where there are strong Protestant congregations, the children of Protestant families are exempt if they attend their own services.

Within Mondema Circuit of the Evangelical United Brethren Church, two groups of people interested in Christianity became Roman Catholic when Roman Catholic schools were opened in their respective towns. When Iye Vande, a Mende-literate woman converted at Mongere, returned to her home ten miles from Mondema, she began preaching the Gospel to many surrounding villages. As the congregations closer to her town grew, she went less far afield. But, unknown to any Evangelical United Brethren officials or missionaries, in several of the far towns and villages groups of people became interested in Christ. Just before I was stationed at Mondema the Roman Catholics opened schools in two of the towns, and the people accepted the leadership of the teachers who were sent.

The Evangelical United Brethren officials, not being alert to church growth opportunities, lost those two towns. If village congregations had been firmly established in them before the opening of the schools, the schools would have made little difference. The Roman Catholics, following their policy of opening as many schools as possible in as many places as possible, harvested the fruits of unrecognized Protestant labors.

# CHAPTER 19

# CONCLUSION

Much church and mission activity is occurring in Sierra Leone, but with little result. Only 4.8 per cent of the population is Christian. Yet large segments of the people are ripe for harvesting into the Kingdom of God. The discussions on the Churches have brought out many factors relating to church growth. Were these to be learned and put into practice, notable church growth could result.

## SALIENT POINTS

The salient points in church growth strategy discussed in the foregoing chapters are outlined below. Common to all is the failure of the school approach to win the tribespeople.

A. Creole Churches
   1. The school approach succeeded in Christianizing the Creoles. It helped produce people movements among them.
   2. The Creoles failed to plant tribal churches because of the culture gap caused by education. To succeed, their outreach must become tribal.
   3. Later generation Christians are not being evangelized.
B. Methodist Church
   1. Widely separated mission stations and far-flung evangelism often result in poor follow-up. Thus the Limba and Temne missions failed.
   2. Statistics are God's tool to help Churches and Missions discover responsiveness. Increases in catechumen enrollments are excellent indicators. But for churches to grow, catechumens must be brought into full membership. Many catechumens enrolled, but many of them were not baptized and were later lost.
   3. The greatest growth has been in people movements. Chris-

tianity has followed the web of family relationships within villages.

4. Growth is smaller than the opportunities allow for, shown by the fact that despite responsiveness growth has stopped in several places where the Christians are still in the great minority. One reason for this is that evangelism is restricted to paid catechists.

5. Greater growth would probably occur if
   a. unpaid itinerators (Class II leaders) were enlisted to help evangelize their own villages and others, and
   b. criteria for ascertaining the readiness of persons to be baptized and brought into membership were re-examined.

6. The vernacular training schools provide leaders better equipped to meet the tribespeople at their level.

7. Static or declining membership indicates that children of believing parents are either not coming to full membership or are leaving the area after finishing school.

8. Methodist organization and use of local preachers (Class I leaders) is excellent.

C. Evangelical United Brethren Church

1. The high one-level ordained ministry is not meeting the spiritual needs of outstation churches because:
   a. ordained ministers are few,
   b. the villages cannot support highly educated men,
   c. the sacraments do not become a vital and indigenous part of the life of such churches, and
   d. highly educated ministers are often as culturally removed from the tribespeople as are Creoles.

2. Schools and ecclesiastical machinery reduce constructive supervision and church growth.

3. The power structure needs to be altered giving more authority to leaders at lower levels.

4. A two-level ministry is needed and should be introduced by ordaining Class III leaders (evangelists) who are able pastors and church planters.

5. The greatest church growth is in people movements, begun in prayer and itineration, and continued by organizing village congregations into sections and parishes, and training volunteer leaders. Greater harvesting would occur if
   a. the Church concentrated on ripe areas, even if it meant deploying evangelists from static churches and stationing missionaries with full supervisory authority, and

    b. when a parish became too large it would start new ones on its edges.

6. This Church should support and use the Methodist Mende training schools. Vernacular-trained leaders are greatly needed.

7. Benevolences have made a few people dependent on the mission, and their operation has been restricted too much to missionaries and institutions. A change in emphasis should be made by

    a. social service through overseas missions becoming the servant of the national Church by helping the local churches do these services in ways possible to them, and

    b. evangelism geared to multiplying local churches — the primary aim of missions — receiving a greater portion of missionary personnel and funds.

D. United Brethren in Christ Church·

1. Ordination of Class III leaders does not of itself produce church growth.

2. Ordained Class III leaders trained and sent to plant churches would probably do so.

E. American Wesleyan Methodist Church

1. Stations and outstations do not occupy a field or prevent other religions from entering. Only numerous village congregations actively engaged in winning others to Christ do.

2. The vernacular Bible school is providing needed evangelists and pastors.

F. Seventh-day Adventist Church

1. The emphasis on Christian education and systematic weekly teaching in the villages with prepared teaching aids is excellent, but the lesson material should be adapted to African culture.

2. The Adventists, with their tight organization, could become church planters. If they become mainly another school planting mission they will play an insignificant part in Christianizing Sierra Leone.

G. Assemblies of God Church

1. The emphasis on a complete break with the past helps prevent syncretism and nominalism.

2. Emotion, as well as intellect, is used to praise God and yields zealous Christians and full participation in worship services.

3. The Christians have firm faith in the power of God to heal.

God heals directly and through scientific medicine. Christians should be taught to use western medicine and a simple biblical reliance on prayers, anointing with oil, and laying on of hands.

## RECOMMENDATIONS

### Church Growth Desired

All the Churches and their assisting Missions desire church growth, and are disturbed when they feel growth is not occurring as rapidly as it ought. But they often feel the Church is growing as fast as it can under existing circumstances, and thus are lulled into complacency. However, the cases cited in the various Churches and many others show that not external circumstances but church and mission programs and policies are preventing growth. For the Church to grow, for tribespeople to be won, for village congregations to be multiplied throughout the land, definite plans, based on careful scrutiny of accurate statistical data and an understanding of social structure and tribal religion, need to be made and carried out. The following points must be considered in such plans.

### Leadership

1. Sierra Leone has two levels of society: the educated few in the large towns, and the nonliterate, nonwestern populace in the villages and small towns. Each level requires ministers trained for its own needs. The present pattern in some of the Churches, e.g., Methodist and Evangelical United Brethren, of a one-level ordination is western and does not meet the needs of Sierra Leone. Each level must have ordained ministers. Only thus can the sacraments become indigenous to village congregational life. In Fiji the Methodist Church (Australian) has two syllabuses. "Syllabus R — Rural Church" trains ministers to serve rural churches. "Syllabus A — Academic" trains ministers to serve the more acculturated churches and in administrative positions. Neither syllabus is western, both are Fijian.

2. Volunteer mature leaders ought to be sought in village congregations and town churches and trained to aid in

church expansion. The nonliterates should be trained in vernacular Bible schools.

3. The general lay membership needs to be revived and challenged to engage in winning others to Christ and to help in planting other churches. This requires a higher level of Sunday School teaching with relevant materials, concentrated instruction, such as the annual Taiama Parish Church Life Institute, and active follow-up.

4. At all these levels of leadership the goal should *not* be general preaching in the hope that some may be converted, but specific labor to the end that whole families and whole villages may be won to Christ. Leaders should think, preach, persuade, and pray with this specific goal in mind.

*Harvesting*

As sections of the population are discovered which are ripe for conversion, and as people in them begin to move to Christ, concentrated effort should be made to place enough harvesters in such areas that all the harvest may be gathered in and strong vigorous churches may emerge in every village throughout the land. If necessary, evangelists and missionaries working in nonresponsive areas should be temporarily deployed to help in the harvest.

*Marriage*

Patterns of marriage for Christians ought to be revised so that Christian homes may be established. Tribal Churches in Sierra Leone should not require that marriages be registered with the government, but provide a ceremony whereby couples who have been married according to tribal custom may vow before God and the congregation to be faithful to each other and establish Christian homes.

Abstinence from polygamy should not be required as evidence of conversion or as necessary for baptism and reception into full membership.

*Requirements for Baptism and Church Membership*

Training for baptism and church membership varies widely from Church to Church, from five days to two years. The

Churches are fairly uniform, however, with respect to requirements of faith. Symbols and practices of the old religious life — for example, pagan or Muslim charms, sacrifices, and rites — are to be rejected. Faith is to be in God through Christ alone. However, if something is not provided to replace the things given up, the old practices will creep back. This is one reason for the importance of making the sacraments an integral, indigenous part of each local church.

Baptism and communion are not rewards for being good, but means of improving Christian life. Therefore, as soon as a person, or group of persons, has turned from the old way to Christ and understands his new relationship to God — a sinner saved by grace and committed to following God's way — he should be baptized and be permitted to commune. Training before baptism should be as much as can be given without keeping groups from being baptized; but whether pre-baptismal training is short or long, it should be followed by continued, systematic, post-baptismal training.

Ever before the Christian must be the goal of a life completely dedicated to God, a life in which the power of the Holy Spirit is evident in holiness and in zeal to help other people and win them to Christ. We work toward such a goal through a continuous proces of perfecting within the Church. Full sanctification ought not to be a requirement for baptism and church membership.

*Missionary Churches*

Missionaries have been and are necessary for church growth in Sierra Leone. When the Creole Churches failed to reproduce across the cultural gap, only the use of missionaries from outside the country enabled some churches to be planted in the interior. More evangelistic missionaries should come. Bishop Neill's statement that Older Churches should plunge ahead to evangelize the tribes if the Younger Churches fail to see their missionary task must be heeded.

Self-propagation, along with self-government and self-support, has long been a goal of all missionary societies when striving to establish indigenous Churches. Despite this, what often happens is the emergence of a Church organized to care for existing churches, but not to carry out systematically the discipling of the tribes. Expansion is usually left to missionaries, and when they are withdrawn discipling often slows down or stops. Lack of sufficient trained ministers to care adequately for existing churches may aggravate this situation.

The goal of missionary societies is to establish missionary Churches with the zeal, organization, and personnel required for them to evangelize their own people. Some Churches have achieved this; for example, the Batak Church in Indonesia. None of the Churches of Sierra Leone has. They can best achieve it in the Batak way — by each local church becoming missionary and making concrete plans to evangelize non-Christian villages. As leaders emerge and are trained, the personnel become available for the Sierra Leone Churches to send out their own missionaries.

Care must be taken, however, that as leaders become educated they do not become detribalized. This is particularly true of those educated to become Class IV leaders — the leaders who will govern the Churches. Leaders must remain in full, sympathetic contact with the people of the land.

## A PLAN FOR WINNING THE MENDE TRIBE

Applying the principles discussed in this book, I propose the following plan, in outline form, for winning the Mende tribe to Christ. I have limited myself to the Evangelical United Brethren Church, although the plan could apply to the other two Mende Churches (Methodist and United Brethren in Christ) as well. In fact, the three Churches ought to form a joint committee with the sole purpose of making bold plans to disciple the Mende tribe. The committee could begin its planning by studying the following outline.

A. Concentration on the ripe chiefdoms.
  1. A missionary stationed in each of the two ripe areas, Mongere and Mondema.
  2. Temporary deployment of evangelists from unripe areas to the two ripe areas.
  3. Special training in people movement methods for these evangelists as well as for others already working in the ripe areas.

B. Lay participation.
    1. Lay training institutes for teaching people movement evangelism to the natural leaders among the new Christians.
    2. Mobilization of the laymen of all the churches, and recruiting of volunteers to become Class II leaders.
    3. Special training for outstanding lay leaders.

C. Local leadership officially installed.
    1. Officially installing the "proved" leadership.
    2. Returning the deployed evangelists to their former areas where they can use the methods they have seen successful and begin group movements to Christ.

D. Church organization — with training for each level.
    1. Class leader of a village congregation.
    2. Section leader of a cluster of village congregations.
    3. Ordained parish pastor of a cluster of sections. This position to be held by an evangelist until he can be replaced by a section leader from within the parish who can be trained for ordination.
    4. Circuit or supervising minister of a cluster of parishes. This position to be held by a missionary until he can be replaced by one of the parish pastors.
    5. Self-support from the beginning, on each level, except for the initial stages of steps 3 and 4 above, when temporary leaders are used.

E. Church membership requirements.
    1. Official enrollment of catechumens by the parish pastor, assisted by the section and class leaders. Adults, by families and villages, to be sought for group enrollment. Individuals accepted only as a last resort, and then encouraged to win their families.
    2. Training of catechumens by village class leaders, with periodic check-ups by the section leader and the parish pastor, using a catechism with essential doctrines simple enough for the catechumen to both learn and share with others.
    3. Candidates for baptism recommended by the village congregation.
    4. Baptism of candidates performed by the parish pastor, assisted by the section and class leaders.
    5. Communicant membership to follow baptism immediately.
    6. Discipline administered by the village congregations, with periodic check-ups by the section leader and the parish leader.

F. Concentration on other chiefdoms, as they ripen in the same manner.
  1. The Kono tribe bordering on the Mondema area.
  2. The Mende and Temne chiefdoms bordering on the Tai-ama-Kori chiefdom, the Mongere-Valunia chiefdom, and the two chiefdoms in the Mondema Circuit.

G. Great, annual, interdenominational gatherings for each section of the tribe, for enthusiasm, inspiration, instruction, and conversion.

H. This program to be followed until the Mende and adjacent tribes are thoroughly discipled with strong missionary congregations in all villages of every chiefdom.

God has given the Church in Sierra Leone several ripe areas which can be used to win the country for Christ. Islam is coming in and the harvesting season will soon pass. God is waiting for the Churches of Sierra Leone to rise to the challenge. We dare not delay.

# BIBLIOGRAPHY

## BOOKS AND ANNUALS

Allen, Roland
 1913 *Missionary Methods, St. Paul's or Ours?* New York, Fleming H. Revell Co.
 1927 *The Spontaneous Expansion of the Church and the Causes Which Hinder It.* London, World Dominion Press.
 1960 *The Ministry of the Spirit: Selected Writings.* David M. Paton, ed. London, World Dominion Press.
Boyd, Andrew and van Rensburg, Patrick
 1962 *An Atlas of African Affairs.* New York, Frederick A. Praeger.
British Information Service
 Nov. 1960 *Sierra Leone: The Making of a Nation.* I.D.1371.
Carter, Charles W.
 1946 *A Half Century of American Wesleyan Missions in West Africa.* Syracuse, New York, Wesleyan Methodist Pub. Assoc.
Cooksey, J. J. and McLeish, Alexander
 1931 *Religion and Civilization in West Africa.* London, World Dominion Press.
Davis, J. Merle
 1943 *How the Church Grows in Brazil.* New York, International Missionary Council.
Emmerich, Henry
 1965 African Statistics. In *The Word in the World.* Techny, Illinois, Divine Word Publications.
Fage, J. D.
 1962 *An Introduction to the History of West ,Africa.* Cambridge, University Press.
Foster, Raymond S.
 1961 *The Sierra Leone Church: An Independent Anglican Church.* London, Society for Promoting Christian Knowledge.
Freetown: Central Office of Information
 1961 *Sierra Leone.*
Fyfe, Christopher
 1962 *A History of Sierra Leone.* London, Oxford University Press.
 *A Short History of Sierra Leone.* London, Longmans, Green & Co.
Grimley, John B. and Robinson, Gordon E.
 1966 *Church Growth in Central and Southern Nigeria.* Grand Rapids, Eerdmans.
Groves, C. P.

1954   *The Planting of Christianity in Africa.* London, Lutterworth Press.

Harris, W.
1950   *The Idea of God Among the Mende.* In *African Ideas of God: A Symposium.* Edwin W. Smith, ed. London, Edinburgh House Press.

Johnson, T. S.
1953   *The Story of a Mission — the Sierra Leone Church: First Daughter of the Church Missionary Society.* London, Society for Promoting Christian Knowledge.

Latourette, Kenneth Scott
1936   *Missions Tomorrow.* New York, Harper & Bros.
1943   *A History of the Expansion of Christianity,* Vol. 5. New York, Harper & Bros.

Lewis, Roy
1954   *Sierra Leone: A Modern Portrait.* London, Her Majesty's Stationery Office.

Little, K. L.
1951   *The Mende of Sierra Leone.* London, Routledge & Kegan Paul, Ltd.

Malinowski, Bronislaw
1954   *Magic, Science and Religion and Other Essays.* Garden City, Anchor Books, Doubleday.

McGavran, Donald A.
1955   *The Bridges of God: A Study in the Strategy of Missions.* New York, Friendship Press.
1965   ed., *Church Growth and Christian Mission.* New York, Harper & Row.

Mendelson, John
1962   *God, Allah & Juju: Religion in Africa Today.* New York, Thomas Nelson & Sons.

Mills, J. S.
1898   *Mission Work in Sierra Leone, West Africa.* Dayton, Ohio, United Brethren Publishing House.

Murdock, George P.
1959   *Africa: Its Peoples and Their Culture History.* New York, McGraw-Hill.

Neill, Stephen
1957   *The Unfinished Task.* London, Edinburgh House Press.

Nevius, John L.
1958   *Planting and Development of Missionary Churches.* Philadelphia, Presbyterian and Reformed Publishing Co.

Newcomb, Harvey
1854   *Cyclopedia of Missions.* New York, Harper & Bros.

Nida, Eugene A.
1960   *Message and Mission.* New York, Harper & Bros.

Parsons, Robert T.
1950   *The Idea of God Among the Kono of Sierra Leone.* In *Afri-*

*can Ideas of God: A Symposium*. Edwin W. Smith, ed. London, Edinburgh Press.
1964 *Religion in an African Society*. Leiden, E. J. Brill.
Phillips, A. (ed.)
1953 *Survey of African Marriage and Family Life*. London, Oxford University Press.
Porter, Arthur T.
1963 *Creoledom*. London, Oxford University Press.
Proceedings of the Church Missionary Society. 1816.
Read, William R.
1965 *New Patterns of Church Growth in Brazil*. Grand Rapids, Eerdmans Publishing Co.
*Sierra Leone Year Book 1964*. Freetown Daily Mail.
Smith, Edwin W.
1928 *The Golden Stool: Some Aspects of the Conflict of Cultures in Modern Africa*. New York, Doubleday, Doran.
Taylor, John V.
1963 *The Primal Vision*. London, Student Christian Movement Press.
Thompson, George
1859 *Thompson in Africa*. Dayton, Ohio, by author.
Trimmingham, J. Spencer
1959 *Islam in West Africa*. Oxford, Clarendon Press.
Vicedom, G. F.
1961 *Church and People in New Guinea*. World Christian Books No. 38, United Society for Christian Literature. London, Lutterworth Press.
Webster, Douglas
1964 *What Is Evangelism?* London, Highway Press.
*Wesleyan Methodist Missionary Society*, Vol. 4. 1922.
*West African Conference Journal*. Evangelical United Brethren Church.
Wold, Joseph
1968 *God's Impatience in Liberia*. Grand Rapids, Eerdmans.
*World Christian Handbook 1957, 1962*. London, World Dominion Press.

ARTICLES, REPORTS, AND PERIODICALS

Busia, K. A.
1959 "Ancestor Worship." Practical Anthropology 6:23-28.
1963 Census of Population, Sierra Leone: Advance Report. Freetown: Central Statistics Office, June 1964. Mimeographed.
Consultation on Theological Education in the South Pacific, Area Reports: No. 10 — Fiji. May 7-14, 1961. Mimeographed.
Loewen, Jacob A.
1964 "The Choco and Their Spirit World." Practical Anthropology 11:97-104.
McGavran, Donald A.
1965 "Social Justice and Evangelism." World Vision 9:7-8, 26.
Nida, Eugene A.
1960 "Religion: Communication with the Supernatural." Practical Anthropology 7:97-112.

1963    "The Church and Its Ministries." Practical Anthropology 10: 233-236.
1965    "Culture and Church Growth." Practical Anthropology 12:22-37.
Pratt, S. A. J.
1965    "Spiritual Conflicts in a Changing African Society." The Ecumenical Review 8:154-162.
Reyburn, William D.
1959    "Polygamy, Economy, and Christianity in Eastern Cameroun." Practical Anthropology 6:1-23.
Shearer, Roy E.
1965    "The Evangelistic Missionary's Role in Church Growth in Korea." International Review of Missions 54:462-470.
Sierra Leone Government
       Report of the Ministry of Education for 1965.
Taylor, John V.
1965    "Beyond the Fringe." C.M.S. Newsletter November.
Tippett, Alan R.
1960    "Probing Missionary Inadequacies at the Popular Level." International Review of Missions 49:411-414.
1966    "Church Growth or Else." World Vision 10:12-13, 28.

## UNPUBLISHED MATERIAL

"Annual Letter of the Committee to the Sierra Leone District Synod," Methodist Church.
File of correspondence between Sierra Leone and the Evangelical United Brethren mission board in Dayton, Ohio.
Minutes of the annual sessions of the United Brethren in Christ Church in Sierra Leone.
"Synod Minutes of the Methodist Church — Sierra Leone."
Interviews with missionaries, African leaders, and members of village congregations in Sierra Leone.

# INDEX

217

Trimmingham, J. Spencer, 47
Tucker, Thomas, 136

United Brethren in Christ (UBC),
33, 69, 83, 115, 183, 185, 206,
210; Ch. 11
United Christian Council (UCC),
82, 120, 201
United Methodist Church, 97,
103, 104
United Nations, 31
United States, 7, 16, 27, 143
University College of Sierra Leone;
*see* Forah Bay College

Vai tribe, 29, 48
Vande, Iye, 202
vernacular training, 150, 152, 160,
166, 183, 185, 205, 206; *see* Bible
school, Mende; Bible school,
Temne; catechism, Mende; *and*
Women's Training Centre

Wars, tribal, 25
Waterloo, 96
web movement, 160

Wesleyan Educational and
Theological Institution, 89
Wesleyan Methodist Church,
97, 104
Wesleyan Methodist Missionary
Society, 67, 68, 86, 92, 97,
99, 116
West, the (Western ethos), 20, 33,
38, 51, 53, 89, 140, 143, 147,
152, 168, 178, 207
West African Methodist Church,
103, 104
Western Area, 25, 27, 31, 75
West Indies, 28, 89
Williams, Henry, 168
Wold, Joseph C., 61, 105, 111,
166, 168
Women's Training Centre, 120, 166
Wundi Society, 159

Yaounde, Cameroun, 140, 141
Yalunka tribe, 47, 70, 81, 97
Yieleh, 94
Yoni Chiefdom, 30
Yoni-Sherbro, 142
York Island, 94
Yoruba tribe, 27, 28, 81, 105